The New Encyclopedia of Knitting Techniques

The New Encyclopedia of Knitting Techniques

A comprehensive visual guide to traditional and contemporary techniques

Lesley Stanfield & Melody Griffiths

RUNNING PRESS
PHILADELPHIA • LONDON

A QUARTO BOOK

ISBN: 978-0-7624-4086-3

Library of Congress Control Number: 2010925948

Conceived, designed, and produced by
Quarto Publishing plc
The Old Brewery
6 Blundell Street
London N7 9BH

QUA: EKT2

TEXT EDITORS: Eleanor Van Zandt, Claire Waite
PATTERN CHECKER: Sue Horan
ILLUSTRATORS: Ch'en Ling, Jenny Dooge
PICTURE RESEARCHER: Laurent Boubounelle
INDEXER: Pamela Ellis

CREATIVE DIRECTOR: Moira Clinch
PUBLISHER: Paul Carslake

Color separation by Pica Digital Pte Ltd, Singapore
Printed by 1010 Printing International Ltd, China

Running Press Book Publishers
2300 Chestnut Street
Philadelphia, PA 19103-4371

Visit us on the web!
www.runningpress.com

CONTENTS

INTRODUCTION

Knitting is the art of constructing a flexible fabric from a notionally continuous thread. The surface of the fabric can be smooth or textured, and the knitted pieces can be flat or tubular, straight or shaped, in infinite variety. Chapter One contains all the essential information you need to get started, from the basic skills of how to work knit and purl stitches to techniques for shaping and embellishing your knitting, as well as practical advice for creating your own designs. Chapter Two features a collection of more than 150 traditional and original stitch patterns—explore, experiment, and adapt them to create knitting that is all your own work.

Symbols, such as a black dot to indicate reverse stockinette stitch, are used to explain textured stitch patterns.

These richly patterned Peruvian hats are recent examples of an old tradition.

Ideas for motifs can be found everywhere—from old prints to antique textiles.

Color patterns are shown as color charts.

Customize patterns with simple embellishment techniques such as beading or embroidery.

CHAPTER ONE

Knitting Skills

There is very little you need to know about knitting to get started—knit and purl are the only two stitches to learn. It is then simply a case of combining them in different ways to produce different effects. This chapter features practical guidance and step-by-step instruction for a wide range of knitting techniques.

EQUIPMENT

YOU DO NOT NEED COMPLICATED OR EXPENSIVE EQUIPMENT TO LEARN TO KNIT—JUST KNITTING NEEDLES AND YARN. AS YOU PROGRESS IN THE CRAFT, YOU CAN COLLECT MORE EQUIPMENT AS YOU NEED IT.

To experiment with different yarns and gauges, you will need knitting needles in different sizes. You will also need a cable needle for working cable stitch patterns, and double-pointed needles or a circular needle if you want to try knitting in the round.

When you are ready to knit a garment, you will need a tape measure or ruler, stitch holders, scissors, a tapestry or yarn needle, and maybe a few other items of equipment.

ESSENTIAL EQUIPMENT
Knitting needles are an investment because you will use them time and time again. Look after your needles carefully and they will last for years, but when the points are damaged or the needles are bent, it is time to throw them out and buy new ones.

DOUBLE-POINTED NEEDLES
Double-pointed needles are sold in sets of four or five, and in several lengths. They were traditionally made of steel, but aluminum needles are more usual now, with bamboo and plastic in some sizes.

CIRCULAR NEEDLES
Circular needles are simply two short needle ends joined by a flexible nylon or plastic cord. The length of a circular needle is measured from needle tip to needle tip. Most sizes are in lengths of 16in (40cm) to 47in (120cm).

STRAIGHT KNITTING NEEDLES
Pairs of needles are made in a variety of lengths, ranging from around 10in (25cm) to 16in (40cm). Most knitting needles are aluminum, usually with a pearl-gray finish, though some are nickel-plated. Larger needles are made of plastic to reduce their weight. Bamboo needles are a flexible alternative.

NEEDLE GAUGE
This knitting needle gauge has metric sizes on one side and imperial on the other.

TAPE MEASURE
The most useful tape measures have both inches and centimeters on the same side, so that you can compare measurements.

SCISSORS
Choose scissors that are not too small and not too large, but very sharp.

SEWING NEEDLES
You will need blunt-pointed needles—either tapestry or yarn needles—in different sizes for different weights of yarn.

KNITTER'S THIMBLE
Worn on the index finger of the hand that holds the yarn, this is used for managing multiple lengths of yarn in stranded color knitting.

BOBBINS
Bobbins are used to prevent multiple lengths of yarn from tangling together during intarsia color knitting.

CABLE NEEDLES
These are used for knitting cable stitch patterns. Some have a kink or crank to help keep the stitches on the needle.

OTHER USEFUL ITEMS
You will find some of these knitter's notions indispensable.

POINT PROTECTORS
Little point protectors stop the stitches from falling off the needles if you have to leave your knitting in the middle of a row.

ROW COUNTER
A row counter helps keep your place.

CROCHET HOOK
A crochet hook can be used to rescue dropped stitches as well as to bind off.

FINALLY, FOR FUN
Though not strictly necessary, pompon rings and a knitting bobbin are great for getting children interested in handling yarn; they also make short work of creating decorative extras.

YARNS

FEELING THE YARN AS IT SLIPS THROUGH YOUR FINGERS IS ONE OF THE PLEASURES OF KNITTING. ADD TO THAT ENJOYMENT BY EXPLORING A WHOLE RANGE OF YARNS, FROM FINE AND SMOOTH TO BULKY AND TEXTURED, IN SYNTHETIC BLENDS AND NATURAL FIBERS.

Yarn is presented either as a ready-wound ball or a wind-it-yourself hank. The fiber content and construction determine how much yarn you get for the weight, so two balls that weigh the same may be very different sizes or contain very different lengths of yarn. Whatever you choose, buy the best you can afford, and your knitting will last.

Alpaca yarn

Bamboo yarn

Cotton yarn

Lambswool and alpaca yarn

Mohair and silk yarn

Wool and cotton yarn

Merino wool yarn

Handspun tweed yarn

Wool and cotton yarn

SMOOTH YARNS

Sometimes called classic yarns, these smooth yarns in wool, cotton, or mixed fibers are the knitter's reliable friends. However fine or thick these yarns are, they will always show up stitch patterns beautifully.

TEXTURED YARNS

Fibers such as alpaca, silk, and linen make yarns that look smooth in the ball but have a distinct character when knitted. Mohair and angora can be used alone or mixed with other fibers for a soft and fluffy surface. Flecked and marled yarns give a tweedy effect, while roving yarns are single-ply and loosely twisted, giving a handspun look.

Fur-effect
yarn

Eyelash
yarn

Ribbon
yarn

KNITTING WITH RIBBON TRIM
It is possible to knit with ribbon trim, but ribbon yarns tend to be more flexible and easier to knit with than the ribbon you would use as trim. Ribbon trim may not be very hard-wearing or launder well, and it is also more expensive than ribbon yarn.

Self-striping
sock yarn

Yarn from
recycled
fabric

SPECIALTY YARNS
Some yarns are designed for a specific purpose, such as for knitting socks. Sock yarns are often fine-weight, and they may have elastin, nylon, or both added to produce socks with a snug fit. Self-striping and hand-dyed yarns are particularly popular for knitting socks.

Multicolored
yarn

IMPROVISED YARNS
Experiment with string or raffia; rip strips of cotton fabric and join them with knots; or cut spirals from cloth, plastic sheeting, or mock leather or suede, and sew the ends together. If you can make a continuous thread out of it, you can knit with it.

Raffia and
string

Bouclé
yarn

NOVELTY YARNS
Also called fashion yarns, these change from season to season—one year tweedy bouclés fill the stores; next time you look everything is metallic. Chenille's velvety texture is a perennial favorite, but it is worth trying them all—from shiny ribbon yarns to richly textured blends.

Cord

GETTING STARTED

Using medium-size needles and a smooth, medium-weight pure wool yarn, practice the steps on the following pages and soon you will be knitting smoothly and rhythmically.

HOLDING YARN AND NEEDLES

KNITTING IS A TWO-HANDED CRAFT IN WHICH STITCHES ARE WORKED OFF THE LEFT NEEDLE AND ONTO THE RIGHT. TO GET STARTED, SIT COMFORTABLY AND RELAX. KNITTING REQUIRES HAND AND EYE COORDINATION, WHICH IS HARD TO ACHIEVE IF YOU ARE TENSE.

There are many ways to hold and control the yarn and needles, and there is no single correct method. Experiment with those suggested here until you find one that suits you.

HOLDING THE YARN
The yarn runs through and around the fingers, leaving the fingertips free to manipulate the needles and control the yarn. The holds shown below have been devised in order to feed the yarn onto the needle evenly. In each of the holds, the working end of the yarn that feeds onto the needle is over the index finger; the ball of yarn feeds onto the little finger.

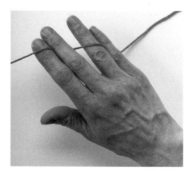

LOOSELY IN RIGHT HAND
To tension the yarn loosely, simply slip the yarn alternately over and under the fingers.

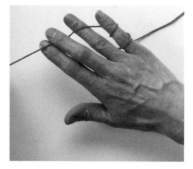

MORE FIRMLY IN RIGHT HAND
To tension the yarn more firmly, wrap the yarn around the little finger, then over and under the other fingers.

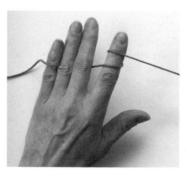

LOOSELY IN LEFT HAND
To tension the yarn loosely, try taking it over the little finger, under the next two, and around the index finger.

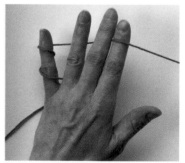

MORE FIRMLY IN LEFT HAND
To tension the yarn more firmly, wrap the yarn around the little finger, then under and over the other fingers.

HOLDING THE NEEDLES

Once you are holding the yarn, pick up a pair of needles, one in each hand, and try out these different holds. Some knitters hold the right needle like a pen; others hold it overhand like a knife. The left needle is usually held overhand. With the free-needle (or pen) hold, the needles used are as short as is practical, and the weight of the knitting on the right needle is supported by the hand and wrist. With the fixed-needle (or knife) hold, long needles are used, and the right needle is tucked under the arm for support.

FIXED NEEDLE WITH YARN IN RIGHT HAND
With your right hand, pick up a needle, hold it overhand like a knife, and tuck the end of the needle under your arm. Take the other needle in your left hand, holding it lightly over the top. Practice moving the left needle against the right. When knitting, you will find that you can let go of the right needle each time you make a stitch.

FREE NEEDLE WITH YARN IN RIGHT HAND
With your right hand, pick up a needle and hold it like a pen. Take the other needle in your left hand, holding it lightly over the top. Try moving the needles forward and back with your fingertips, keeping your elbows relaxed at your sides. When you cast on and start knitting, do not drop the right needle to manipulate the yarn; instead, support it in the crook of your thumb and use your index finger to control the yarn.

YARN IN LEFT HAND
Hold the needle in your right hand like a pen or knife as preferred; hold the needle in your left hand lightly over the top. When knitting, hold the yarn taut with the left hand while hooking or catching it with the point of the right needle.

BASIC CAST-ONS

THE FIRST STEP IN BEGINNING ANY PIECE OF KNITTING IS TO CAST ON SOME STITCHES. HERE ARE THREE OF THE MOST USEFUL WAYS TO CAST ON.

The two-needle cable cast-on makes a strong edge with a rope-like twist, but it is not very elastic. The thumb cast-on uses just one needle and is versatile. It is very compatible with ribs due to its elasticity. Used with garter stitch, it is indistinguishable from the rest of the knitting because it is, in effect, a knit row. The backward loop cast-on also uses one needle; it is simple and useful for buttonholes.

SLIP KNOT

Putting a slip knot on the needle makes your first stitch. You can coil the yarn around your fingers or lay it flat.

1 Coil the yarn into a loop, then bring the strand forward and through the loop. Insert the needle as shown to secure the yarn.

2 Pull one end to tighten the knot, then gently pull the other end of the yarn to close the knot up to the needle. You are now ready to cast on.

CABLE CAST-ON

This cast-on is made by knitting a stitch, then transferring it from the right to the left needle.

1 Leaving a short end, make a slip knot on one needle. Holding this needle in the left hand, insert the other needle into the front of the slip knot. Take the yarn around the right needle and pull through a stitch, then transfer it to the left needle.

2 From now on, insert the right needle between the stitches each time. Transfer each new stitch to the left needle as before.

Tip

A less robust cable cast-on is made if you take the needle into the stitch each time, instead of between stitches. This creates a useful edge for hems.

THUMB CAST-ON

Also known as long-tail cast-on, this method involves simply knitting each stitch off your thumb.

BACKWARD LOOP CAST-ON

Tension the yarn carefully for this cast-on, which is often used at the end of rows.

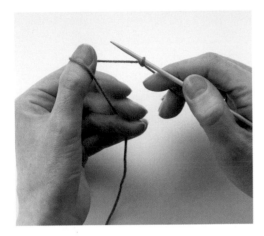 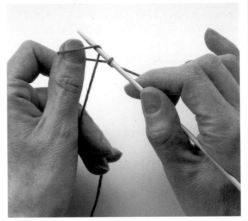 

1 Measure off about three times the length of the edge to be cast on and make a slip knot on the needle. Hold the needle and yarn from the ball in your right hand.

3 Take the yarn around the needle, then draw a loop through to make a stitch. Gently pull the end to close the stitch up to the needle. Repeat until the required number of stitches, including the slip knot, have been cast on.

2 Tensioning the other end of the yarn in your left hand, make a loop around your thumb and insert the right needle into the loop.

Leaving a short end, make a slip knot on the needle. Tension the yarn in your left hand, and make a loop around your thumb. Insert the needle in the loop, slip your thumb out, and gently pull the yarn to make a stitch on the needle.

Tip

Measuring out three times the length of the cast-on edge for the thumb cast-on can be cumbersome when you require a large number of stitches. An alternative method is to use a slip knot to join together the ends from two balls of yarn, then hold one strand with the left hand and the other with the right hand and work the cast-on. Once the required number of stitches has been cast on, discard the yarn in the left hand and continue working with the yarn in the right.

This method can also be used to create a provisional cast-on. A length of smooth contrast yarn is used in the left hand. This is then unpicked and the loose stitch loops are picked up and worked in the other direction.

MORE CAST-ONS

THESE THREE CAST-ONS ARE NOT NECESSARILY MORE DIFFICULT THAN THE BASIC CAST-ON METHODS, BUT THEY WILL EXPAND YOUR REPERTOIRE OF TECHNIQUES TO GIVE YOU MORE OPTIONS IN YOUR KNITTING. ONCE YOU ARE FAMILIAR WITH DIFFERENT CAST-ONS, YOU CAN DECIDE WHETHER TO SUBSTITUTE ONE FOR ANOTHER TO ACHIEVE A PARTICULAR RESULT.

SEE ALSO
- Basic cast-ons, pages 16–17

SELECTING A CAST-ON

The cast-on method you choose depends upon the finished outcome you require—an elastic or firm cast-on, decorative or plain. In some cases, an extra-strong cast-on may be required, such as on children's garments where edges may be prone to hard wear. Interesting cast-on or bound-off edges can also transform a simple garment. For example, the Channel Island cast-on is both strong and decorative, and can look especially good on the edge of collars and cuffs.

The basic skills will take you a long way in knitting, but sometimes the more unusual techniques can make all the difference to the success of your garments. Learning how and when to use alternative techniques is the first step toward designing for yourself.

CHANNEL ISLAND CAST-ON

Strongly defined knots decorate the edge of this robust cast-on. For an odd number of stitches, work as described here. For an even number of stitches, simply cast on one more stitch at the end.

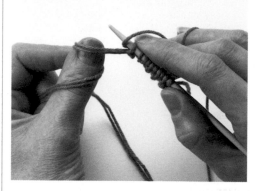

Leaving an end six times the length of the edge to be cast on, put a slip knot on one needle. Double this length back on itself so that the free end hangs down where it meets the needle at the slip knot. Take the doubled end in your left hand and the single strand from the ball in your right hand. Wind the doubled end twice around the thumb of your left hand. Insert the needle up through both of the double strands of yarn on your thumb, then take the single strand around the needle and pull through a stitch. Drop the double strands off the thumb and pull on the ends to bring the knot up to the needle. Bring the single strand forward and then over the needle to make a second stitch. Continue to make pairs of stitches in this way, ending with a stitch knitted from the thumb.

CHANNEL ISLAND CAST-ON
The decorative quality of this cast-on can be seen on the lower edge of a typical Guernsey sweater.

KNOTTED CAST-ON

Casting on by this method makes a small knot at the base of each stitch and gives an attractive double-strength edge.

Leaving an end about four times the length of the edge to be cast on, make a slip knot on one needle. Cast on one stitch using the basic thumb method, then lift the slip knot over the stitch and off the needle. Cast on two more stitches, then lift the first of these over the second and off the needle; repeat for each cast-on stitch required.

KNOTTED CAST-ON

This example has a knot at the base of each cast-on stitch. To vary the result, simply alter the number of stitches cast on before forming a knot.

LONG-TAIL OR CONTINENTAL CAST-ON

This method produces a cast-on identical to the basic thumb cast-on, but it is much faster to work. Start by leaving a tail about three times the length of the desired cast-on edge and then put a slip knot on one needle.

1 Hold the needle in the right hand and both ends of yarn in the left hand. Wrap the tail around the left thumb and loop the other strand around the index finger. Grasp the yarn strands in the palm of your hand with your remaining fingers.

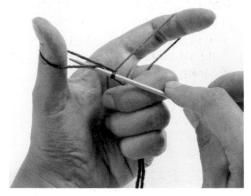

2 Slide the needle up through the loop around your thumb.

3 Take the needle over the top of the yarn on your index finger, and draw this through the thumb loop.

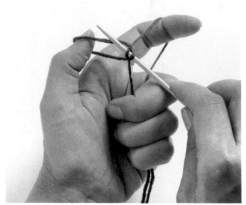

4 Release the thumb loop and tighten it around the needle. Repeat until you have the required number of stitches.

KNIT AND PURL

ONCE YOU HAVE MASTERED THE CABLE CAST-ON, YOU WILL FIND THE KNIT STITCH—THE MOST BASIC OF STITCHES—VERY FAMILIAR. TO PROGRESS TO STOCKINETTE AND OTHER STITCH PATTERNS, YOU WILL NEED TO KNOW HOW TO PURL. PURLING IS NOT DIFFICULT—JUST THINK OF IT AS THE OPPOSITE OF A KNIT STITCH.

SEE ALSO
• Holding yarn and needles, pages 14–15
• Cast-ons, pages 16–19

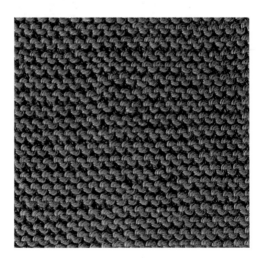

GARTER STITCH
This stitch pattern uses only knit stitches, so it is perfect for beginners. It is an excellent stitch pattern for many novelty and hand-dyed yarns.

MAKING A KNIT STITCH
Hold the yarn and needles in whichever way feels most comfortable to you.

1 Insert the right needle into the first stitch on the left needle. Make sure that it goes from left to right into the front of the stitch.

3 Using the tip of the right needle, draw a loop of yarn through the stitch.

KNITTING A ROW
Continue making stitches on the right needle until all stitches have been worked off the left needle, then transfer the needle with the stitches to the left hand to work the next row. You will soon find that the movements flow into each other as you pick up more speed.

2 Taking the yarn behind, bring it up and around the right needle.

4 Slip the stitch off the left needle. There is now a new stitch on the right needle.

GARTER STITCH
Knitting every stitch of every row produces a stitch pattern known as garter stitch. Garter stitch makes an elastic fabric in which the stitches are stretched widthwise, while the rows draw up to give an almost square gauge. Although it is very simple, this reversible fabric can be very versatile. Knitted loosely, it is soft and springy. Worked firmly, the fabric lies flat, which makes it useful for bands and borders.

MAKING A PURL STITCH

Hold the yarn and needles in the same way as for making a knit stitch.

1 Insert the right needle into the first stitch on the left needle. Make sure that it goes into the front of the stitch from right to left.

2 Taking the yarn to the front, loop it around the right needle.

3 Lower the tip of the right needle, taking it away from you to draw a loop of yarn through the stitch.

4 Slip the stitch off the left needle. There is now a new stitch on the right needle.

PURLING A ROW

In the same way as when knitting a row, continue purling stitches on the right needle until all stitches have been worked off the left needle. Then swap the needles so that the needle with the worked stitches is in the left hand and the empty needle is in the right hand, ready to work the next row.

Purl stitch is actually just a knit stitch worked from the other side of the fabric, so if you purl every stitch of every row, the result will be garter stitch.

Tip

To count rows in garter stitch, count each ridge as two rows. To count rows in stockinette stitch, count the ridges on the reverse of the fabric.

STOCKINETTE STITCH
The best-known combination of knit and purl is called stockinette stitch. It is very simple—just knit one row and purl one row alternately.

REVERSE STOCKINETTE STITCH
The right side of stockinette is smooth and the other side is ridged. If you use the ridged side as the right side of the piece, it is called reverse stockinette.

BINDING OFF

BINDING OFF—ALSO CALLED CASTING OFF—LINKS STITCHES TO MAKE A NEAT EDGE THAT WILL NOT UNRAVEL. ALTHOUGH THERE IS ONE BASIC METHOD OF BINDING OFF, THERE ARE SIMPLE VARIATIONS THAT CAN ALSO BE USEFUL.

Chain bind-off is the easiest and most used method. The decrease bind-off is less well known, but gives a very smooth finish. Binding off with a crochet hook makes it easy to cope with slippery yarns or tight stitches.

These illustrations show binding off on the right side of stockinette, but you can also bind off on a wrong-side row or in knit and purl, depending on the stitch pattern.

CROCHET BIND-OFF

This bind-off can be as tight or as loose as necessary, according to the tensioning of the crochet chain.

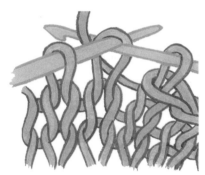

Holding the needle in your left hand, slip the first stitch onto the hook. Insert the hook into the next stitch, catch the yarn, and pull it through both stitches, dropping both stitches from the needle and hook as you do so. Insert the hook into the next stitch and repeat. When you reach the last stitch, break the yarn, and pull it through.

STORING YOUR KNITTING

When storing a piece of knitting that is not yet ready to be bound off, it may seem sensible to slide the needles through the ball of yarn to keep everything safely together, but this is best avoided because it could damage the yarn fibers.

CHAIN BIND-OFF

Lifting one stitch over the next makes a chain along the top of the knitting on the side the bind-off is worked.

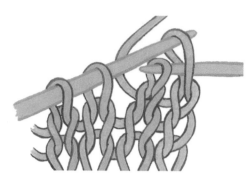

1 Start by knitting the first two stitches. Use the point of the left needle to lift the first of these stitches over the second stitch and off the needle.

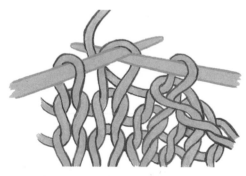

2 Knit the next stitch so that there are two stitches on the right needle, then lift the first over the second. Repeat until there is one stitch left. Break the yarn, draw it through the stitch, and pull it tight.

CHAIN BIND-OFF

This bind-off has been worked loosely. This makes the edge more elastic.

DECREASE BIND-OFF

This bind-off does not make a chain, so it is useful for a rib edge. Try alternating knit two stitches together and purl two stitches together.

1 Knit the first two stitches together, then slip the stitch just made onto the left needle.

2 Knit together the first two stitches on the left needle—the one already worked and the next one. Slip the stitch just made onto the left needle, as before. Repeat until one stitch is left. Break the yarn, draw it through the stitch, and pull it tight.

DECREASE BIND-OFF

This bind-off takes a bit longer to work than chain bind-off, but the result is decorative and elastic.

PICOT BIND-OFF

This bind-off produces a decorative edge. The picots can be made on every stitch, in which case the edge will flute, or they can be spaced with as many chain bind-off stitches between as needed to make the edge lie flat.

Insert the right needle into the first stitch on the left needle, and knit a stitch but do not slip the stitch off the left needle. Slip the new stitch onto the left needle, then make a second new stitch as before. Use the chain bind-off method to bind off four stitches, then slip the remaining stitch back onto the left needle. Repeat along the row, making two stitches and binding off four each time.

PICOT BIND-OFF

In this example, the picots have been made alternately over an odd number of stitches.

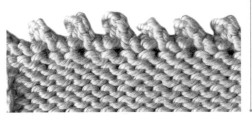

THREE-NEEDLE BIND-OFF

Instead of joining back and front shoulder edges by binding them off separately and sewing them together, a softer join is made if the two sets of stitches are bound off together using a third needle. This can be done invisibly on the wrong side, as shown here, or made into a feature by binding off on the right side.

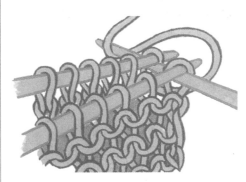

1 Do not bind off the shoulder stitches, but leave them on spare needles. Place the back and front shoulders right sides together, with the needles pointing in the same direction. Using a third needle, knit the first stitch on the near needle together with the first stitch on the back needle.

2 Knit the next pair of stitches together, and then take the first stitch on the right needle over the second, in the usual way for a chain bind-off. Continue until all the stitches have been bound off. When binding off two pieces of knitting with wrong sides together to make a feature on the right side of the fabric, make sure that the chain edge of the bind-off faces the same way on each shoulder.

ESSENTIAL TO KNOW

This section features essential information for using your newfound knitting skills to make something.

READING PATTERNS

READING A KNITTING PATTERN MAY BE UNFAMILIAR AT FIRST, BUT AS SOON AS YOU HAVE CRACKED THE CODE, YOU WILL BE ABLE TO FOLLOW INSTRUCTIONS WITH CONFIDENCE.

You have found your dream design, but how can you be sure that your sweater will fit? What should you buy? What do pattern abbreviations and repeat instructions mean?

WHAT ARE THE MEASUREMENTS?

The sizes will be set out in sequence, as a grid or with larger sizes in brackets. Fit varies from one design to another, so first compare the actual bust or chest measurement with your body measurement, then check the length and sleeves. Some garments are designed to fit closely, while others are very loose—choose the fit you want.

WHAT DO YOU NEED TO BUY?

It is important to buy the yarn specified. Another yarn, however similar, may not behave in the same way and you might need a different amount. Make sure that you buy enough yarn and check that you have everything else listed, such as a cable needle.

OLD KNITTING PATTERNS
Old knitting patterns can be fascinating, even though the yarn may no longer be available and the style may not be from this season's runway.

SEE ALSO
• Gauge, page 26
• Key to patterns, pages 140–141

CHECKING YOUR GAUGE

Gauge is given as the number of stitches and rows, usually counted over a 4in (10cm) square, worked in a specified stitch pattern on the recommended needle size. The needle size should be treated as a guide only—you may need to use a different size to knit to the gauge given in the instructions.

UNDERSTANDING ABBREVIATIONS

Once you are familiar with abbreviations, you will find it quicker and easier to find your way around the instructions. Some abbreviations are simply the first letter of the word, such as "k" for "knit." Others use the first few letters, such as "rep" for "repeat." Sometimes the first letters of several words are run together— "skpo" for "slip one, knit one, pass the slipped stitch over." Not all knitting instructions use the same abbreviations. For instance, "k1b" may mean "knit in the back of the stitch" or "knit in the row below." It is therefore important to read the abbreviations each time you follow a new set of instructions.

UNDERSTANDING REPEATS

Knitting is full of repetition. Stitch patterns repeat horizontally across a row and vertically over several rows. These multiples can either be shown on a chart or explained in words. Round or square brackets can be used to enclose instructions that are to be repeated. For example, "[k2, p2] 3 times" is a concise way to write "k2, p2, k2, p2, k2, p2."

Asterisks are also used as markers to indicate a repeat. For example, "rep from * to **" means "repeat the instructions contained between the asterisks the number of times specified." When two parts of a garment share the same instructions, a group of asterisks is used to indicate the sections that are the same and where they differ.

READING CHARTS

CHARTS ARE A VISUAL EXPLANATION OF STITCHES AND ROWS. THEY ARE A VERY EFFICIENT WAY TO CHECK YOUR PLACE IN A PATTERN REPEAT OR TO COMPARE ONE REPEAT WITH ANOTHER. EACH SQUARE USUALLY REPRESENTS ONE STITCH. A KEY WILL BE PROVIDED TO EXPLAIN THE COLORS OR SYMBOLS.

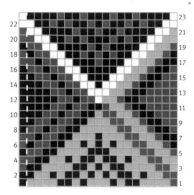

COLOR CHARTS
When working from a color chart, look not only at the sequence of stitches to come but also the color of the stitches in the row below. This makes it easier to place the colors accurately as well as to spot errors.

Charts are always numbered from the bottom to the top, because this is the direction of the knitting. The first row may be either a right- or a wrong-side row. Right-side rows are read from right to left; wrong-side rows are read from left to right. The multiple of the pattern repeat is sometimes shown underneath the chart, while shaded areas or dotted lines indicate extra or end stitches.

Enlarging a chart by photocopying can make it easier to follow. Make several copies and glue or tape them together. If it helps, draw any shapings on the photocopy.

COLOR KNITTING CHARTS

Most color knitting is in stockinette, so every right-side row is knit and every wrong-side row is purl, with the squares on the chart showing the color to be used. The chart may be printed in color or may use a symbol for each color. If any textured stitches are used, they will be shown as symbols and explained in the key.

CHARTS WITH SYMBOLS

Every stitch and every row is shown as on the right side of the knitting. A blank square represents knit on a right-side row and purl on a wrong-side row—making stockinette. A dot represents purl on a right-side row and knit on a wrong-side row—making reverse stockinette. Some symbols represent more than one stitch, such as a decrease. Where the stitch count varies within a stitch pattern, solid areas compensate for the missing stitches. Not all methods of charting use the same symbols, so always check the key.

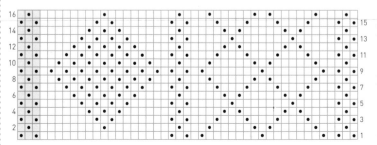

CHARTS WITH SYMBOLS
The stitches in white indicate the repeat. This pattern has a multiple of 42 stitches plus 3 stitches. The additional 3 stitches center or balance the pattern and are represented by the tinted blocks. They are not repeated.

GAUGE

THE GAUGE OF A PIECE OF KNITTING IS THE NUMBER OF STITCHES AND ROWS COUNTED OVER A GIVEN MEASUREMENT. GAUGE IS CONTROLLED BY THE TYPE OF YARN, THE SIZE OF THE NEEDLES, AND THE STITCH PATTERN. ACCURATE GAUGE IS CRUCIAL TO A SUCCESSFUL RESULT.

A knit designer will establish the number of stitches and rows needed to obtain a given measurement—usually 4 inches or 10 centimeters—in the chosen yarn and stitch pattern, and use that information when calculating the size and shape of a garment. It is vital for the knitter to work to the same gauge, otherwise the garment simply will not measure the same.

Knitting patterns emphasize that you must use the correct yarn, but this does not apply to the needle size. The recommended needle size is a guide only; it does not matter what size needles you use as long as you achieve the correct gauge. The same yarn with a different needle size or type of needle can produce a different-sized swatch. Even your mood or how you hold your needles can change the gauge. It is therefore essential that you knit a swatch and check the gauge before starting on the real thing. It is the only way to save wasting time and effort, creating a knit that does not fit.

MEASURING
Use a tape measure or metal ruler to check you have the correct gauge.

> **Tip**
> *The yarn ball band often gives the manufacturer's recommended stockinette gauge, but you should always check your gauge in the specified stitch pattern as well.*

HOW TO MEASURE GAUGE
Knit a swatch using the needle size given in the instructions. Always add a few extra stitches and work a few more rows, because the edge stitches will be distorted. Check the making up instructions and, if necessary, press the swatch. Measure the gauge on a flat surface.

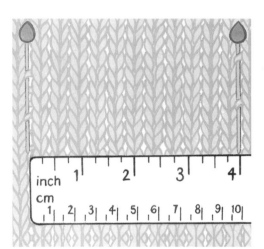

1 Count and mark the stitches with pins, then measure between the pins. If the measurement is correct, you will know that your finished garment will be the right width. If your marked stitches measure less, you are knitting too tightly and the garment will be too narrow. Knit another swatch using larger needles, and measure again. If the marked stitches measure more than they should, you are knitting loosely and the garment will be too wide. Knit another swatch on smaller needles, and measure again.

2 Mark the number of rows and check the measurement. If it is correct, go ahead and start knitting. If the marked rows measure less, your knitting is tight and the garment will be too short. Try using larger needles for your next swatch. If the marked rows measure more, your knitting is loose and the garment will be too long. Try knitting another swatch using smaller needles.

TROUBLE SHOOTING

AS WELL AS KNOWING THE BASIC STITCHES, YOU MUST BE ABLE TO RECOGNIZE AND CORRECT MISTAKES IN YOUR WORK. THESE TIPS WILL HELP YOU GET OUT OF TROUBLE—AND AVOID GETTING INTO TROUBLE IN THE FIRST PLACE.

Tip

Twisted stitches are made when the yarn has been taken the wrong way around the needle to knit or purl. They are also made when stitches are dropped and put back onto the needle the wrong way around. To correct, slip the twisted stitch onto the right needle so that the right leg of the stitch loop is at the front and then slip it back onto the left needle, ready to be worked.

PICKING UP A DROPPED STITCH

Do not panic if you drop a stitch. Simply stop as soon as you can, and use the needles or a crochet hook to pull the unraveled strands through to remake the stitches.

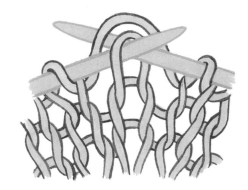

If the stitch has dropped just one or two rows, lift the dropped stitch and the first unraveled strand onto the right needle. Use the left needle to take the stitch over the strand. Repeat if necessary, then lift the new stitch onto the left needle, making sure that it faces the correct way.

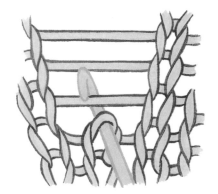

If the stitch has dropped more than one or two rows to form a ladder, insert a crochet hook through the dropped stitch from the front, catch the first unraveled strand, and pull it through to make a new stitch. Each strand of the ladder is a row, so make sure that you catch them all. Put the last stitch onto the left needle.

CORRECTING MISTAKES

The technique of picking up dropped stitches can also be used to fix stitches that have been worked incorrectly on previous rows. Identify which stitch on the needle is immediately above the error, and then knit to a position just to the right of it. Drop the next stitch off the left needle—that is, the stitch above the error—and then ease each loop out of the stitch until you reach the error. Correct the error and pick up the stitches again.

Several stitches can be dropped at the same time, so a wrongly crossed cable can also be corrected. It is often only necessary to drop half the cable stitches as far as the row of the cross, then reposition the stitch loops either in front or behind the other half of the cable and pick up the stitches again.

This works well for many mistakes and is often worth trying before ripping back rows of work. However, it is very difficult on lace stitch patterns or on stranded color knitting.

JOINING IN NEW BALLS OF YARN

Problems such as uneven fabric thickness and distorted stitches can arise if new balls of yarn are joined in the middle of the row. Ideally, start a new ball of yarn at the beginning of a row, where the edge will be part of a seam. Make a neat bundle with the tail end of yarn left from the old ball. To join the new yarn, make a single overhand knot. When sewing up, undo the knot, thread one end onto a sewing needle, and run it through a few stitches of the seam.

SINGLE DECREASES

DECREASES HAVE TWO BASIC FUNCTIONS—THEY CAN BE USED TO REDUCE THE NUMBER OF STITCHES IN A ROW, SUCH AS IN ARMHOLES AND NECKLINES, OR THEY CAN BE COMBINED WITH INCREASES TO CREATE STITCH PATTERNS. A SINGLE DECREASE REDUCES THE WIDTH OF THE KNITTING BY ONE STITCH AT A TIME.

SHAPING

One of the joys of knitting as opposed to sewing is that there is no cutting out. You knit the pieces you need, shaping the fabric at the same time as you are creating it. Decreases make the fabric narrower, while increases make it wider.

FULLY FASHIONED

Single increases and decreases are used to shape sleeves, armholes, and necks. They can be both practical and decorative. Fully fashioned shapings are made several stitches in from the edges, so that the increases and decreases become a visible feature of the design. Shapings can also be used across a row; for example, stitches may be increased or decreased at the top of a rib.

RIGHT-SLANTING SINGLE DECREASES

The two decreases below create a slope to the right on the knit side of the fabric.

KNIT TWO STITCHES TOGETHER (K2 TOG)

Knitting two stitches together on a knit row makes a smooth shaping, with the second stitch lying on top of the first.

1 Insert the right needle through the front of the first two stitches on the left needle, then take the yarn around the needle.

2 Draw the loop through and drop the two stitches off the left needle.

PURL TWO STITCHES TOGETHER (P2 TOG)

For a decrease worked on a purl row that slants to the right on the knit side of the fabric, purl two stitches together.

SOCK WITH AFTERTHOUGHT HEEL

Socks of all shapes and sizes use decreases to create a basic tube shape. An afterthought heel can be worked after the rest of the sock has been completed by cutting a strand of yarn at the heel position, unpicking half a round of stitches, and slipping the upper and lower loose loops onto needles. The loops are then worked to match the toe shaping, using pairs of single decreases on either side of the heel until about third of the original stitches remain. The heel and toe openings are grafted together using Kitchener stitch.

LEFT-SLANTING SINGLE DECREASES

The following four decreases create a slope to the left on the knit side of the fabric.

SLIP-KNIT-PASS SLIPPED STITCH OVER (SKPO)

Worked on a knit row, this method creates a slope to the left, with the first stitch lying on top of the second.

1 Insert the right needle knitwise through the front of the first stitch on the left needle, and slip it onto the right. Knit the next stitch.

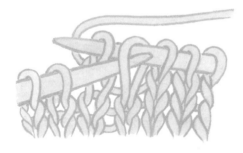

2 Use the tip of the left needle to lift the slipped stitch over the knitted stitch and drop it off the right needle.

SLIP-SLIP-KNIT (SSK)

This is another popular left-slanting single decrease that is worked on a knit row, although it often causes some confusion. Work to the position of the decrease, insert the right needle knitwise through the front of the first stitch on the left needle, and slip it onto the right needle. Repeat this with the next stitch on the left needle, then insert the left needle through both slipped stitches from left to right so that the left needle is in front of the right needle. Knit the two stitches together. This produces a very neat decrease that looks like a left-slanting version of knit two stitches together.

PURL TWO STITCHES TOGETHER THROUGH BACK OF LOOPS (P2 TOG TBL)

For a decrease worked on a purl row that slants to the left on the knit side of the fabric, purl two stitches together through the back of the loops.

SLIP-SLIP-PURL (SSP)

This single decrease is also worked on a purl row to create a slope to the left on the knit side of the fabric. Work to the position of the decrease, insert the right needle knitwise through the front of the first stitch on the left needle, and slip it onto the right. Repeat this with the next stitch on the left needle. Slip the stitches back onto the left needle without twisting them again. Then, using the right needle, purl the two stitches together through the back of the loops.

BALANCED SINGLE DECREASES

Choosing the correct decrease for the stitch pattern is vital for shaping garments successfully. Working single decreases in pairs produces some interesting decorative effects that are commonly exploited in lace stitch patterns and armhole shaping.

NORMAL DECREASE

For a smooth line of shapings, work a left-slanting decrease near the beginning of the row, and a right-slanting decrease near the end.

FEATHERED DECREASE

For a feathered line of shapings, work a right-slanting decrease near the beginning of the row, and a left-slanting decrease near the end.

DOUBLE DECREASES

SOMETIMES IT IS NECESSARY TO DECREASE SEVERAL STITCHES TOGETHER RATHER THAN WORK A SERIES OF SINGLE DECREASES.

A double decrease shapes the knitting more rapidly. In single rib, a double decrease can be placed so that the pattern is not interrupted on the following row. In many stitch patterns, double decreases are used with double increases to create beautiful lacy effects.

All decreases can be adapted to make multiple decreases by taking more stitches together, but it is very important to be aware of the position of the stitch that lies on top. Always pair a left-slanting and a right-slanting decrease when shaping a garment or working a stitch pattern. The dominant center stitch of the balanced double decrease makes a design feature of shaped darts and gives a clean line to lace patterns.

BALANCED DECREASES AT SIDES
To balance decreases at each side of the fabric, as shown here, work rib 5, then knit 3 together at the beginning of the row. At the end of the row, slip 1, knit 2 together, pass the slipped stitch over, rib 5. The decreases reduce three stitches to one each time, so that the rib pattern remains correct on the following rows.

Tip
Purling several stitches together is a lot easier than knitting them together, so try to finish off large bobbles with a purl stitch.

RIGHT-SLANTING DOUBLE DECREASES
The two decreases below create a slope to the right on the knit side of the fabric.

KNIT THREE STITCHES TOGETHER (K3 TOG)
Worked on a knit row, the stitch farthest to the left will lie on top, giving a decrease that slants to the right.

Insert the right needle into the front of the third stitch, then through the fronts of the other two stitches. Take the yarn around the needle in the usual way, draw the loop through, and drop the three stitches off the left needle.

PURL THREE STITCHES TOGETHER (P3 TOG)
For a double decrease worked on a purl row that slants to the right on the knit side of the fabric, purl three stitches together. Insert the right needle into the fronts of the next three stitches, take the yarn around the needle in the usual way, draw the loop through, and drop the three stitches off the left needle.

LEFT-SLANTING DOUBLE DECREASES
The two decreases below create a slope to the left on the knit side of the fabric.

SLIP ONE, KNIT TWO TOGETHER, PASS SLIPPED STITCH OVER (SK2PO)
Worked on a knit row, the slipped stitch is passed over a single decrease.

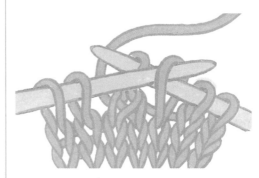

Slip the first stitch knitwise, knit the next two stitches together, then lift the first stitch over as shown. The first stitch lies on top, so the decrease slants to the left.

PURL THREE STITCHES TOGETHER THROUGH BACK OF LOOPS (P3 TOG TBL)
For a double decrease worked on a purl row that slants to the left on the knit side of the fabric, purl three stitches together through the back of the loops.

BALANCED DOUBLE DECREASE

Working a double decrease that takes one stitch from each side and leaves the center stitch on top has lots of potential for shaping and for working beautiful stitch patterns.

1 Insert the right needle into the second and first stitches as if to knit two together, and slip these stitches onto the right needle.

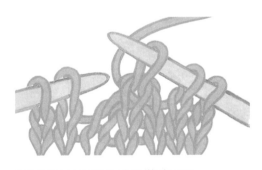

2 Knit the next stitch, then lift the two slipped stitches over it. The center stitch of the decrease will lie on top.

BALANCED DECREASES AT CENTER

In this swatch, the ribs travel to the center and the decreased stitches are neatly hidden under the center stitch. The rib remains correct for the following rows.

PICKING UP STITCHES

THIS TECHNIQUE IS VITAL FOR A WELL-FINISHED GARMENT BECAUSE IT ELIMINATES BULKY SEAMS. TRY TO MAKE IT AS NEAT AS POSSIBLE.

Picking up stitches simply involves knitting up new stitches along an edge, ready to work a band or border in another direction.

To pick up a given number of stitches along an edge, fold it in half, mark the halfway point, then fold each half and mark the quarters. Divide the required number of stitches by four, and pick up this number of stitches evenly from each marked quarter.

HOW TO PICK UP A STITCH

For an even finish, use a slightly smaller needle than was used to knit the project previously and pick up stitches at regular intervals.

PICKING UP ALONG A STRAIGHT EDGE
The secret of a satisfactory picked-up edge is to pick up the right number of stitches. When picking up from row ends, do not work into every row end or the band will flare. Skip row ends at regular intervals so that the band will lie flat. To pick up along a cast-on or bound-off edge, work into every stitch.

With the right side facing you, insert the needle under an edge stitch, take the yarn around, and pull a loop through to make a stitch. Repeat for each required stitch. Remember that the next row will be a wrong-side row.

PICKING UP ALONG A SHAPED EDGE
Do not skip stitches along the shaped edges of a neckline; work into every decrease and row end. When picking up from a stitch pattern, space stitches as necessary to fit in with the pattern.

SINGLE INCREASES

INCREASES HAVE TWO FUNCTIONS. THEY CAN BE USED TO INCREASE THE NUMBER OF STITCHES IN A ROW, SUCH AS IN CHEST SHAPING AND TOP-DOWN YOKES, OR COMBINED WITH DECREASES TO CREATE STITCH PATTERNS. A SINGLE INCREASE ADDS TO THE WIDTH OF THE KNITTING BY ONE STITCH AT A TIME.

BAR INCREASES

This single increase makes a little bar on the knit side of the fabric at the base of the new stitch. This makes it easier to the count rows between rows with shaping.

KNIT INTO FRONT AND BACK OF STITCH (INC OR KF&B)

Knitting into the front and back of a stitch is the most common increase.

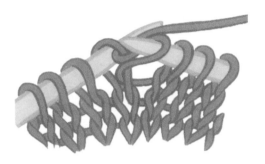

1 Knit into the front of the stitch and pull the loop through, but leave the stitch on the left needle.

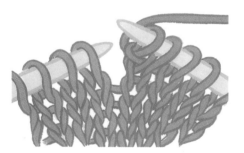

3 Slip the stitch off the left needle, making two stitches on the right needle. Note that the bar of the new stitch lies on the left.

PURL INTO FRONT AND BACK OF STITCH (INC OR PF&B)

You can also work a bar increase by purling into the front and back of a stitch.

BALANCED SINGLE INCREASES

If you work a bar increase into the first stitch in a row, the increase will appear one stitch in, so the edge will be smooth. Make the increase at the end of the row in the last stitch but one, and the bar will also sit one stitch in from the edge. Lifted-strand increases can be made the same number of stitches in from each edge. Perfectionists will turn the strand in the opposite direction at each end of a row.

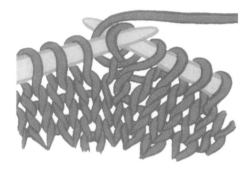

2 Knit into the back of the stitch on the left needle.

BALANCED BAR INCREASES

These bar increases have been worked so that they look as if they are three stitches in from each edge. However, because of the nature of the bar increase, there is one more stitch after the increase on the left edge.

LEFT-SLANTING LIFTED-STRAND INCREASES

Both of the single increases below create a slope to the left on the knit side of the fabric.

STRAND OR MAKE ONE LEFT ON A KNIT ROW (M1 OR M1L)

Making a stitch from the strand between the stitches is a very neat way to increase—it is almost invisible. It is also useful for shaping in color knitting.

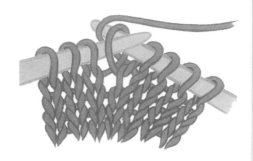

Use the left needle to pick up the strand between the stitches on the needles from the front. The right leg of the lifted strand should be at the front of the left needle. Knit into the back of it to make one new stitch.

STRAND OR MAKE ONE LEFT ON A PURL ROW (M1 OR M1L)

For an increase worked on a purl row that slants to the left on the knit side of the fabric, use the left needle to pick up the strand between the stitches on the needles from the back. The right leg of the lifted strand should be at the front of the left needle. Purl into the back of it to make one new stitch.

RIGHT-SLANTING LIFTED-STRAND INCREASES

Both of the single increases below create a slope to the right on the knit side of the fabric.

STRAND OR MAKE ONE RIGHT ON A KNIT ROW (M1 OR M1R)

This increase has all the advantages of left-slanting lifted-strand increases, but it slants to the right instead. Use the left needle to pick up the strand between the stitches on the needles from the back. The left leg of the lifted strand should be at the front of the left needle. Knit into the front of it to make one new stitch.

STRAND OR MAKE ONE RIGHT ON A PURL ROW (M1 OR M1R)

For a decrease worked on the purl row that slants to the right on the knit side of the fabric, use the left needle to pick up the strand between the stitches on the needles from the front. The left leg of the lifted strand should be at the front of the left needle. Purl into the front of it to make one new stitch.

YARN OVERS

The most common type of increase used in lace patterns such as this scarf is an open increase known as a yarn over. The yarn is simply taken over the needle to form a new stitch, leaving a lace hole beneath. Yarn overs are often paired with a decrease stitch, so that the fabric remains the same width.

BALANCED LIFTED-STRAND INCREASES

If you are shaping at the sides of a garment, work lifted-strand increases one or more stitches in from each edge, allowing the same number of stitches before and after the increase. If you are shaping a dart, leave one or more stitches between increases.

DOUBLE INCREASES

HERE ARE TWO NEAT WAYS TO INCREASE TWO STITCHES AT A TIME RATHER THAN WORK A SERIES OF SINGLE INCREASES.

Double increases are useful for lace stitches and for keeping stitch patterns, such as ribs, correct while shaping.

WORKING TWICE INTO A YARN OVER

If your instructions tell you to make two stitches from a double yarn over on the previous row, try this neat way of pairing the made stitches.

LIFTED-STITCH DOUBLE INCREASE

Working into each side of the stitch on the row below makes an increase that is decorative and useful for keeping patterns such as rib and seed stitch correct when shaping. This increase can be varied by knitting into the back of the lifted stitch or purling into the lifted stitch.

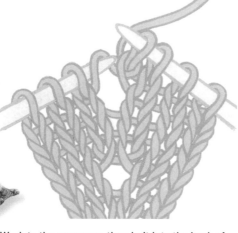

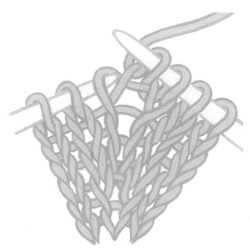

Work to the yarn over, then knit into the back of the loop. Drop the second yarn over off the left needle, then pick it up with the left needle as shown, so that it is turned the other way, and knit into the front of it. The two stitches make a neat inverted V shape over the hole.

Work to the increase, lift the next stitch from the row below onto the left needle, and knit it. Knit the next stitch on the left needle, then lift the stitch previously knitted into back onto the left needle, and knit it again.

DOUBLE INCREASE

Shaping in single rib looks very decorative when lifted-stitch double increases are used. To keep the rib correct, knit into the lifted stitches to make knit stitches, and purl into the lifted stitches to make purl stitches.

Tip

The lifted-stitch method can also be used to increase just one stitch. If you knit the lifted stitch and then the next stitch, the increased stitch will lie to the right. If you knit the next stitch and then the lifted stitch, the increased stitch will lie to the left.

BIAS AND CHEVRON KNITTING

USE INCREASES AND DECREASES WITHIN THE KNITTED FABRIC TO CREATE BIAS AND CHEVRON EFFECTS.

SEE ALSO
• Decreases and increases, pages 28–34

If you increase and decrease one stitch at opposite ends on alternate rows so that the stitch count remains constant, the knitted fabric will slant while the direction of the stitches remains vertical—a technique known as bias knitting.

Decreases at the beginning and increases at the end of a row tilt the fabric to the left; increases at the beginning and decreases at the end tilt the fabric to the right. Although often used to make flexible facings, this principle can also be used to shape knitted fabrics of any size. The examples shown here are in stockinette stitch—the stripes are simply to emphasize the slant—but textured stitch patterns and color motifs can also be shaped in this way. The angle of the slant can be varied by spacing the shapings farther apart.

Put left and right bias shapings together to make a chevron fabric with the stitches fanning out from or traveling into the center. You will need to work a double increase or decrease at the center, or use single shapings each side of one or more center stitches. A single chevron can be used to create a knitted fabric of any size, or you can combine upward- and downward-pointing chevrons to make stitch patterns.

CHEVRON KNITTING

These examples are in stockinette with shaping on every right-side row, but you can vary the spacing of the increases and decreases to suit your stitch pattern.

BIAS KNITTING

To make a flexible bias strip, cast on a few stitches and work the increases and decreases one or two stitches in from each end.

Double increasing in the center
Increasing at each side of the center stitch and decreasing at each end of every right-side row makes the stitches fan out from the center and forms an upward-pointing chevron.

For a slant to the right
Increase one stitch at the beginning and decrease one stitch at the end of each right-side row.

Double decreasing in the center
Double decreasing at the center and increasing at each end of every right-side row makes the stitches travel to the center and forms a downward-pointing chevron.

For a slant to the left
Decrease one stitch at the beginning and increase one stitch at the end of each right-side row.

Tip
Try bias knitting in a stranded color pattern. The motifs will seem to move to the left or right, depending on the shapings.

USEFUL TO KNOW

Once you have mastered the basics of knitting, you can begin to explore some of the additional techniques for creating special effects.

CIRCULAR KNITTING

WORKING IN THE ROUND ON DOUBLE-POINTED NEEDLES WAS PROBABLY THE MOST COMMON METHOD OF KNITTING UNTIL THE END OF THE NINTEENTH CENTURY. TODAY, MANY KNITTERS ARE REDISCOVERING THE ADVANTAGES OF THIS TECHNIQUE.

MEDALLION
This medallion is worked in six sections. The increase is a yarn over made at the start of each section, giving a swirled effect.

In circular knitting, it is possible for the right side of the work to be always facing. It is actually easier to do almost every type of knitting in the round, including cables and especially stranded color patterns. For stockinette stitch, you just knit every round. Ribs and seed stitches are worked in the same way but on an even number of stitches. For garter stitch, you will need to knit and purl alternate rounds. Working from charts is simple; you just read each row of the chart from right to left, omitting any edge stitches.

TYPES OF NEEDLE

Knitting can be worked in the round using double-pointed needles or a circular needle. Double-pointed needles can be bought in sets of four or five needles. Four is the minimum number of needles that can form a round—three needles to hold the stitches and one to knit with. However, you can use as many more double-pointed needles as you need. Circular needles are perfect for knitting larger projects.

In both cases, care should be taken with the first round. Cast on in the usual way, checking that the stitches are not twisted before working the first round. If using double-pointed needles, divide the number of stitches between all but one of the needles.

USING DOUBLE-POINTED NEEDLES

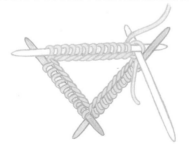

To start, bring the first and last needles together and use the spare needle to knit with. Take care to pull firmly on the yarn each time you work the first stitch on a new needle, or you could leave a ladder of loose stitches.

USING A CIRCULAR NEEDLE

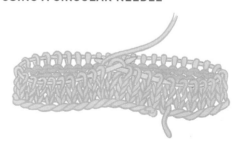

To start, use the needle tip in the right hand to work the stitches on the needle in the left hand. Change to a smaller circular needle or a set of double-pointed needles if the number of stitches decreases and the stitches no longer slide easily around the original needle.

TURNING ROWS

ALSO KNOWN AS SHORT-ROW SHAPING, THIS TECHNIQUE IS USED TO SHAPE THE KNITTED FABRIC WITHOUT BINDING OFF STITCHES UNTIL ALL THE SHAPING IS COMPLETE. THE SHORT ROWS ARE MADE BY TURNING THE NEEDLES PARTWAY THROUGH A ROW, LEAVING SOME OF THE STITCHES UNWORKED.

CREATING A SLOPED EDGE

For a steep slant, leave one or two stitches unworked; leave more for a gentler slope. For symmetrical shaping, leave stitches unworked at both ends. For a smooth transition between rows, wrap the yarn around a slipped stitch to anchor it before turning and working back.

WRAPPING STITCHES

1 Knit the number of stitches needed for the short row, bring the yarn forward, slip the next stitch purlwise, then take the yarn back.

2 Return the slipped stitch to the left needle, ready to turn and work the next short row.

WORKING WRAPPED STITCHES

Once all the short rows have been worked to create the sloped edge, an extra row or two are usually worked into each stitch on the needle. This produces a smoother edge. The loops around the wrapped stitches can either remain untouched, as shown in the photograph below, or the loops can be disguised by working them together with the stitch around which they are wrapped. To do this, work to the first wrapped stitch, insert the right needle under and through the loop, and work together with the next stitch.

SLOPED EDGE

This swatch shows the use of turning rows to make a sloping edge. The stripes help you to see clearly where the yarn is taken around the slipped stitches. The same technique can be used when turning on a purl row.

BEADS AND SEQUINS

KNITTING BEADS OR SEQUINS INTO THE FABRIC GIVES SOME VERY EXOTIC RESULTS. THEY CAN BE WORKED ALL OVER THE FABRIC, IN A REGULAR PATTERN, OR AT RANDOM.

SEE ALSO
• Joining in new balls of yarn, page 27

THREADING

The beads or sequins must be threaded onto the yarn before being knitted into the fabric. If possible, buy beads or sequins ready-strung, tie the fine nylon thread to the end of the yarn, and slide them onto the yarn. Thread an estimated quantity, and when these are used up, break the yarn and thread a fresh quantity. Do this at the end of a row, and join in the new yarn in the usual way.

To thread loose beads, take a piece of fine wire about 2in (5cm) long, lay the end of the knitting yarn across it, then bend it in half. Twist the two ends of wire together and thread the beads.

SLIPPING BEADS

The easiest way to knit with beads is the slip stitch technique, which can be used for almost any size of ornament. It is worked on the right side of stockinette stitch.

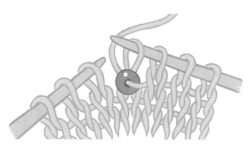

Knit to the stitch where you want the bead, and bring the yarn to the front. Slide the bead along the yarn, and push it firmly up against the needle. Slip the stitch purlwise, take the yarn to the back, and knit the next stitch. This leaves the bead suspended in front of a stitch.

SEQUINED KNITTED FABRIC
Sequins are flexible and can be pushed through a stitch more easily than beads. Closely worked beads or sequins can be used for bands and edgings as well as the whole fabric.

KNITTING SEQUINS

Sequins can also be worked by the slip stitch technique, but they lie better if they are worked into a stitch. This is done on the wrong side of stockinette stitch.

Purl to the stitch where you want the sequin, insert the needle, take the yarn around the needle in the usual way, then slide a sequin down to the needle. Complete the purl stitch, pushing the sequin through to the right side of the work. Secure the sequin on the next row by knitting into the back of the stitch.

BEADED KNITTED FABRIC
Beading alternate stitches on alternate rows gives this allover effect. Slip several stitches to accommodate a large bead or bugle bead.

SLIP STITCH COLOR KNITTING

IF YOU WANT TO CREATE MULTICOLORED KNITS BUT ARE WORRIED ABOUT HANDLING MORE THAN ONE COLOR YARN AT A TIME, THEN SLIP STITCH COLOR PATTERNS ARE THE ANSWER BECAUSE ONLY ONE COLOR IS USED IN A ROW.

GINGHAM MOUSE
The trousers of this charming knitted mouse are worked in gingham check.

These patterns are an easy way to create color effects, because the slip stitches are slipped to take the color over two rows—you do not need to strand colors along the row. For a reversible pattern, you may need to work two consecutive rows in the same direction, so use a circular needle or double-pointed needles in order to slide the stitches along to work from the other end.

Gingham check

> MULTIPLE OF 4 STITCHES PLUS 2

Stitches are purled on all wrong-side rows, so this pretty check looks like stranded color knitting. When choosing colors for a true gingham effect, yarn A should be the medium tone.

Colors A, B, and C.
Cast on with A
Row 1 (RS): Using A, k.
Row 2: Using B, p2, [sl 2 wyif, p2] to end.
Row 3: Using B, k2, [sl 2 wyib, k2] to end.
Row 4: Using A, p.
Row 5: Using C, sl 2 wyib, [k2, sl 2 wyib] to end.
Row 6: Using C, sl 2 wyif, [p2, sl 2 wyif] to end.
These six rows form the pattern.

Spotted stripes

> MULTIPLE OF 4 STITCHES PLUS 1

By slipping stitches and sliding at row ends, you can achieve the effect of spots in the stripes. On the other side, the colors are reversed. After the first few rows, it is very easy to keep your place in this pattern.

Circular needle. Colors A and B.
Cast on with A, slide.
Row 1: Using B, p1, [k1, p1, sl 1 wyib, p1] to end, turn.
Row 2: Using B, k1, [sl 1 wyif, k1, p1, k1] to end, slide.
Row 3: Using A, k1, [p1, k1] to end, turn.
Row 4: Using A, p1, [k1, p1] to end, slide.
Row 5: Using B, p1, [k1, sl 1 wyif, k1, p1] to end, turn.
Row 6: Using B, k1, [p1, sl 1 wyib, p1, k1] to end, slide.
Row 7: Using A, as 3rd row, turn.
Row 8: Using A, as 4th row, slide.
These eight rows form the pattern.

LOOPS

MAKING AN EVEN, LOOPED PILE OVER THE SURFACE AS YOU KNIT IS A FASCINATING PROCESS. MUCH OF THE FINAL EFFECT DEPENDS ON THE TYPE OF YARN USED AND WHETHER THE LOOPS ARE CUT OR UNCUT.

Loops are usually worked on alternate rows so that they all lie on the right side of the fabric. The density depends on whether the loops are made with one or more strands of yarn and whether they are worked on every stitch or on alternate stitches. Experiment with these two techniques to decide which suits your yarn.

SINGLE LOOPS

This is a very secure loop that can be cut without unraveling. It is made on right-side rows of stockinette or garter stitch.

1 Knit a stitch, but do not slip it off the needle. Bring the yarn to the front between the needles; take it clockwise around your left thumb and back between the needles. Knit the stitch on the left needle again and slip it off in the usual way.

2 Insert the left needle into the front of the two new stitches on the right needle and knit them together through the back of the loops. When the knitting is finished, the loops can be cut or left uncut.

DOUBLE LOOPS

Clusters of loops can be made on wrong-side rows of garter stitch. These clusters consist of two loops, but you can make triple loops in the same way. Do not cut these loops.

Insert the needle into the next stitch as if to knit, but take the yarn over the right needle and first two fingers of the left hand twice, then over the needle again. Draw through, making three loops on the right needle. Insert the left needle into the loops and knit into the back and front of them to make two stitches on the right needle. Lift the first stitch over the second and off the needle. This locks the loops fairly securely.

DOUBLE LOOPS
These loops have been worked in a textured stretch yarn for a close-pile surface.

SINGLE LOOPS
These loops have been worked in cream wool and cut to give a sheepskin effect.

TUCKS AND PLEATS

KNITTED FABRICS NEED NOT BE FLAT. YOU CAN MAKE THREE-DIMENSIONAL EFFECTS LIKE TUCKS AND PLEATS WITHOUT USING A SEWING NEEDLE.

TUCKS

Tucks are usually worked in stockinette stitch and are similar in construction to a hem. On the right side, fold the knitting along a row and knit each stitch on the needle together with the back loop of each corresponding stitch of a previous row. Stitches can be joined across the row to give a corded effect or to make a casing. You can use small groups of stitches to make bobbles. For a small bobble, turn, work five rows on three stitches, then join by knitting these stitches together with the three of the first row.

MOCK PLEATS

The curl of knit stitches rolling over purl stitches can be used to make a pleated fabric. These stitch patterns are based on rib, so they also make the fabric narrower and longer.

MOCK PLEATS

To knit this kilted pleat effect, refer to the tree and flags pattern in the knit and purl stitch collection. Cast on a multiple of eight stitches and repeat the stitches of one flag pattern only.

TUCKS

From the top, the bobbles are actually small tucks and the cord below them is only four rows deep. The next tuck has a picot edge and the heavier tuck below it has a purl ridge along the fold.

SEE ALSO

• Facings and hems, pages 44–45
• Tree and flags stitch pattern, page 68

TRUE PLEATS

Plan your pleats in stockinette stitch and define the folds with slip stitches on right-side rows. Slip one stitch with the yarn in front for an inside fold; slip one stitch with the yarn at the back for an outside fold. At the top of the pleat, divide the stitches into three—for the face, turn-back, and underside. Slip these groups onto double-pointed needles and turn the needles to fold the fabric. Knit one stitch from each of the three needles together each time to close the top. Baste the pleats before pressing.

TRUE PLEATS

This technique can be used to make knife-edge pleats, box pleats, or inverted pleats.

ENTRELAC

THE ENTRELAC TECHNIQUE LOOKS LIKE MAGIC, WITH THE CHANGING DIRECTION OF THE STITCHES MAKING A WOVEN FABRIC.

Entrelac uses the techniques of turning rows, increasing and decreasing, and picking up stitches to create a patchwork that is actually knitted all in one. Each block has twice as many rows as stitches—the number of stitches used to make the base triangles determines the size of the blocks. You can use any stitch pattern you want, as long as the repeat or motif fits the number of stitches and rows for each block.

SEE ALSO
• Decreases and increases, pages 28–34
• Picking up stitches, page 31
• Turning rows, page 37

BASIC TECHNIQUE

The best way to understand the entrelac technique is to knit up a sample. This swatch of stockinette stitch entrelacs is based on a multiple of 12 stitches. Use any yarn with appropriate size needles, but change color for each row of blocks to emphasize the change in direction of knitting.

STARTING ROW OF BASE TRIANGLES

Using first color, cast on 36 sts.
First base triangle: P2, turn, k2, turn, p3, turn, k3, turn. Purling one more stitch from left needle each time, continue in this way until there are 12 sts on right needle.
Do not turn. Leave these stitches and work two more base triangles.

FIRST ROW OF BLOCKS

Change to second color.
The first row of blocks has side triangles.
First side triangle: K2, turn, p2, turn, kf&b, skpo, turn, p3, turn, kf&b, k1, skpo, turn, p4, turn. Decreasing one stitch from base triangle on knit rows each time, continue until kf&b, k9, skpo has been worked, do not turn, leave these 12 sts.
Block: Pick up and knit 12 sts from row ends of base triangle, turn, p12, turn, k11, skpo, turn, p12. Continue in this way until all sts of base triangle have been decreased; do not turn.
Work a second block between second and third base triangles.
Second side triangle: Pick up and knit 12 sts from row ends of last base triangle, turn, p2 tog, p10, turn, k11, turn, p2 tog, p9, turn, k10. Continue decreasing at beginning of every purl row until 1 st remains, turn, slip st onto left needle.

SECOND ROW OF BLOCKS

Change to first color.

The second row of blocks does not have side triangles.

Block: P1, pick up and purl 11 sts, turn, k12, turn, p11, p2 tog, turn, k12. Continue in this way until all stitches of first row block have been decreased; do not turn.

Work remaining blocks in this way.

MOTIF ENTRELAC

The little boats look as if they are going up and down on the waves because of the different directions of the knitting. The opening and closing triangles are in contrast colors. Each block of this entrelac is worked on 12 stitches and each boat motif is 9 stitches wide, leaving the edges clear for joining the blocks.

CONTINUING TO WORK ENTRELAC

The next row of blocks is the same as the first row of blocks, but working into the second row of blocks instead of base triangles. Alternating colors, work as many rows of blocks as you want, but always end with a first row of blocks, then finish off with triangles to give a straight edge at the top.

LAST ROW OF BLOCKS

Change to first color.

Closing triangles: P1, pick up and purl 11 sts from row ends of side triangle, turn, k12, turn, p2 tog, p9, p2 tog, turn, k11, turn, p2 tog, p8, p2 tog, turn, k10, turn. Continue in this way until turn, k2 has been worked, turn, p1, p2 tog, turn, k2, turn, p3 tog, 1 st remains.

Picking up and purling 11 sts from row ends of blocks, work second and third closing triangles.

ENTRELAC WITH CABLES

Adding a cable to your entrelac is fun. This swatch is based on a multiple of 12 stitches, but to balance the pattern, you will need an extra edge stitch. Increase 1 st on the first row and decrease it on the last row of each block to work this 6-stitch cable with 2 sts in reverse stockinette stitch on each side.

FINISHING DETAILS

Choosing appropriate finishing touches and techniques can make all the difference to the success of your project.

FACINGS AND HEMS

INSTEAD OF WORKING EDGES IN RIB OR GARTER STITCH, YOU CAN MAKE HEMS OR FACINGS FOR A MORE SUBSTANTIAL DOUBLE-FABRIC FINISH.

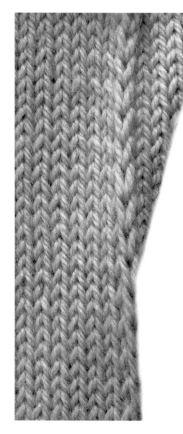

FACING
A line of slip stitches forms a natural fold line for a facing.

The addition of facings or hems really needs to be considered before you start to knit. It is possible to knit from an edge to produce a facing or hem, but there will be a join that may be difficult to disguise. These techniques owe more to dressmaking than to knitting, but they can be very successful if the right design and yarn are chosen.

FACINGS

Unlike ribbon or woven fabric, a knitted stockinette facing will be flexible and a perfect color match. For the front edges of a jacket or cardigan, it is best to work the facing as part of the main piece. To ensure that the facing folds on the same stitch along its length, slip this stitch on every right-side row.

PLAIN HEM

A knitted hem can be turned up and sewn in place in the same way as a woven fabric hem. However, this can be bulky and the folded edge may spread, so it is preferable to make a neat knitted-in hem.

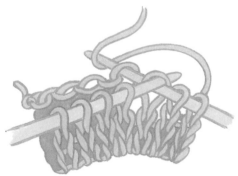

With smaller needles than for the main piece, cast on fairly loosely using the loop method. Work the depth of the hem in stockinette stitch. Mark the fold with a ridge by working a row out of sequence—either three purl rows or three knit rows, the center row of the three making the ridge. Change to the needles for the main piece and continue in stockinette stitch until the depth from the ridge matches that of the hem, ending with a purl row. To join the hem on the next row, fold the hem up behind the main piece, then knit together the first stitch from the left needle with the first stitch from the cast-on edge. Continue in this way to the end of the row.

PICOT HEM

A very attractive way to mark the fold of a hem is to work a row of eyelets that, when the hem is turned up, make a row of well-defined picots. Work to the depth of the hem, ending with a wrong-side row.

If there is an odd number of stitches, work the next row as k1, *yo, k2 tog, rep from * to end. Over an even number of stitches, work the row as k2, *yo, k2 tog, rep from * to end.

PICOT HEM
The stitches between the eyelets form the picots when the hem is turned up.

MITERED CORNERS

Where a hem and facing meet, or between an edging and a front band, a mitered corner may be the neatest solution. For this you need to increase or decrease to make a 45-degree angle. Shaping on alternate rows in garter stitch or seed stitch produces this angle almost perfectly. In stockinette, achieving the correct angle may entail shaping on a mixture of alternate rows and every row, because the stitches are wider than they are tall.

MITERED CORNER
The garter stitch edging and front band form a neatly mitered corner.

FASTENINGS

FASTENINGS ARE DETAILS YOU SHOULD CONSIDER BEFORE YOU START KNITTING AND PERHAPS WORK A SWATCH FOR. IF YOU ARE KNITTING A PROJECT THAT REQUIRES SOME FORM OF FASTENING, HERE IS HOW TO MAKE IT AS NEAT AS POSSIBLE.

BUTTONHOLES WITH A FACING
One buttonhole in the main piece and one buttonhole in the facing come together when the facing is turned in along the line of slip stitches.

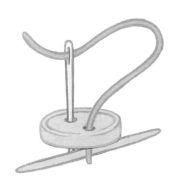

SECURING A BUTTON WITH A SHANK
Faced front edges or a bulky yarn may require the button to have a shank. To make the shank, sew on the button over a spacer such as a cable needle. When the button is secure, remove the spacer, twist the yarn around the shank, then fasten off.

BUTTONHOLES

Buttonholes are best kept simple. Knitted fabric does not lend itself to the detailed finishing used on woven fabric, so try to make buttonholes neat enough so that hand sewing with buttonhole stitch afterward is unnecessary, because this reduces size and flexibility and can be clumsy. Choose the buttons first and make the buttonholes to fit.

EYELET BUTTONHOLES

A single or double eyelet is often sufficient for a small buttonhole. A single eyelet is made with a yarn over and single decrease; a double eyelet is made with a double yarn over and a balanced single decrease on either side.

HORIZONTAL BUTTONHOLES

The simplest method is to bind off stitches on one row with a chain bind-off, and cast on the same number above them on the next row with a backward loop cast-on. To prevent a hole before the first stitch of the cast-on group, work into the front and back of the last stitch before the buttonhole, and cast on one stitch less.

VERTICAL BUTTONHOLES

Knit along the row to the place where the buttonhole will be, turn, then work the required number of rows. Break the yarn, rejoin it where the knitting turned, and work the same number of rows on this side. Finally, work on all stitches to close the buttonhole at the top. Use the two ends of yarn left to reinforce the top and base of the buttonhole.

ZIPPERS

Zippers are slightly incompatible with knitting, but they are sometimes more appropriate than buttons. Edge the zipper opening with a few stitches of garter stitch or seed stitch. Pin and baste the zipper in place, lining up rows or stitch patterns on either side. Open the zipper to back stitch it. For a neat finish, knit narrow facings to cover the zipper tape.

MAKING UP

ASSEMBLING A KNITTED GARMENT INVOLVES TWO PROCESSES—PRESSING OR BLOCKING EACH PIECE OF KNITTING, THEN SEWING THE PIECES TOGETHER.

PRESSING

Pinning out and pressing your knitting before sewing up will make an enormous difference to the finished garment. Always check the ball band for yarn care, and test a sample swatch before applying heat or steam to your knitting—natural fiber yarns are usually quite robust, but man-made mixes can collapse and therefore need a cool, dry iron.

Pin each piece out to size with right side down on a padded board, using a tape measure to check the measurement. Cover the board with a checked fabric to help you line up the rows and stitches. Then lay a dampened cotton muslin cloth on top, and gently apply the iron. Never stamp the iron down or push it along the knitting. Knitting can be molded into shape at the pressing stage if it is wool or cotton. Buy or make a tailor's ham—an overstuffed fabric ball—for pressing set-in sleeve heads.

BLOCKING

If the yarn is delicate or if the stitch pattern is textured, pin out the pieces but do not press. Instead, dampen them with a water spray, then allow them to dry naturally—a process known as blocking.

SEWING UP

This takes time to do properly, so do not be tempted to rush this process. Using small safety pins, long sewing pins—quilter's pins

MATTRESS STITCH SEAM ON STOCKINETTE STITCH
The seam is almost invisible in stockinette stitch.

WEAVING IN YARN ENDS

All pieces of knitting begin and end with a tail of yarn, and more are created when you join in a new ball, change colors, and sew up seams. These yarn ends need to be woven into the wrong side of the knitted fabric using a blunt-ended sewing needle. Most can be woven along a seam, but some may have to be woven in and out of the back of a few stitches. Make sure that they do not show through on the right side of the fabric. Trim any excess yarn.

MATTRESS STITCH

This method, also known as invisible seam or ladder stitch, is good for joining side and sleeve seams in most stitch patterns.

Place both pieces of knitting flat, with right sides facing and the edges to be joined vertical. Thread a blunt-ended sewing needle with yarn and secure at one lower edge—the first side. Take the needle under the cast-on edge of the second side, draw the yarn through, then go under the first cast-on edge again. Tension the yarn to level the edges. Take the needle under the strand between the edge stitch and the next stitch on the first row of the second side, and draw the yarn through. Repeat for the first row of the first side. Continue joining row ends from alternate sides in this way, without splitting stitches.

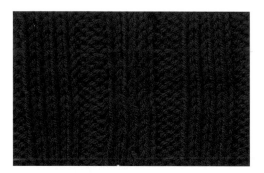

MATTRESS STITCH SEAM ON RIB
Ribbing needs to be planned so that, when the seam is joined, the stitches at each edge combine to make a whole rib.

MATTRESS STITCH SEAM ON STRIPED FABRIC
Stripes and color patterns are easier to match when sewn together from the right side.

are ideal—or a length of contrasting yarn threaded onto a tapestry needle, secure any points that should align on the project. If you are using safety pins, use them horizontally to the edge rather than parallel to the edge—this leaves the fabric more flexible. This can be done with normal pins, but they tend to get in the way if they protrude beyond an edge.

You do not have to use the same stitch to sew up all the seams. Consider each seam carefully and then, in a good light, try to match the edges stitch for stitch along their length. In general, even, regular stitching will be less noticeable. After sewing a project together, lightly press or steam the reverse side of the project again using a damp cloth.

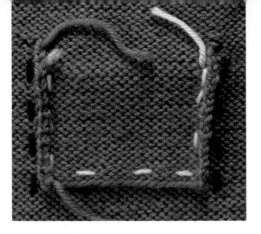

POCKET LININGS
To keep pocket linings square when stitching them down, baste contrast color guidelines between the stitches on each side of the pocket opening on the right side of the fabric. Turn over and follow the basted guidelines to sew the pocket linings down.

NEAT DROP SHOULDERS
If you are joining a straight bound-off sleeve top to the row ends of a back and front to make a drop shoulder, do not match stitch for stitch. Skip a few row ends at regular intervals to compensate for the different stitch and row gauges.

EDGE-TO-EDGE MATTRESS STITCH
This technique is useful for joining shoulders. The stitches run in opposite directions, so the side edges will be a half-stitch out, but this can be hidden in a seam.

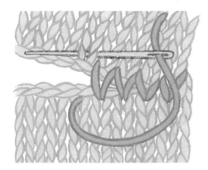

Thread a blunt-ended sewing needle with yarn and bring it up through the center of the first stitch on the front. Take it under the edge stitch on the back, and down through the first stitch again. Repeat, taking in a whole stitch each time to match the front and back stitches perfectly.

SLIP STITCH
Slip stitch is a particularly light way to seam. It is useful for catching down pocket linings as well as to secure facings.

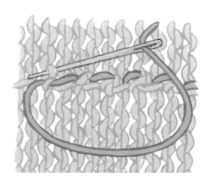

With wrong sides facing, baste the pieces to be joined, matching rows. Thread a blunt-ended sewing needle with yarn. Secure the end, then take the needle alternately under a strand on the main fabric and an edge strand. Do not let the stitches show on the right side or pull the yarn too tight.

BACK STITCH
Back stitch creates a strong seam that is ideal for seams that may need to bear some weight. It is also a useful embroidery stitch.

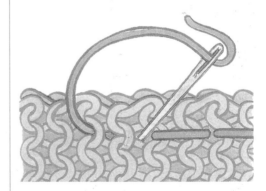

Hold the pieces with right sides together. Thread a blunt-ended sewing needle with yarn and secure it at the right-hand end. Lining up rows and working one stitch in from the edge, bring the needle up through both pieces between stitches of the first and second rows, then down between the first row and cast-on edge. Come up again one or two rows on, and go down next to the previous stitch. Complete the seam in this way, working between the knitted stitches.

KITCHENER STITCH

ALSO REFERRED TO AS GRAFTING OR WEAVING, THIS TECHNIQUE IS USED TO JOIN TWO SETS OF UNBOUND STITCHES TOGETHER WITHOUT CREATING A VISIBLE SEAM. THE TECHNIQUE CAN ALSO BE USED TO ALTER THE LENGTH OF A GARMENT.

Commonly used to join shoulders, Kitchener stitch involves duplicating a row of stitches using yarn and a blunt-ended sewing needle. Always use a blunt needle to avoid splitting stitches. Thread the needle with a length of matching yarn three times the width of the row.

GETTING STARTED

Lay the pieces to be joined close together, with the knitting needles pointing in the same direction and the unbound stitches near the tips so that you can slip them off the needles easily as you trap them with the sewn stitches. The Kitchener stitches should be tensioned to match the knitting, but you can go back once the row has been completed and ease the stitches. It is easiest to Kitchener stitch in stockinette or reverse stockinette stitch, as described here. However, once you understand how to imitate knit and purl stitches, you can using Kitchener stitch to graft pieces in other stitch patterns.

ADJUSTING THE LENGTH OF KNITTED FABRIC

Examine the fabric and look for a discreet place to add or subtract rows. The start or end of a pattern change usually works well. To make the alteration, snip a stitch in the center of the row, then pick up the loops of the stitches above and the stitches of the row below as you ease out the yarn. Use two needles, one to pick up the stitches below and the other for the loops above. Using the two ends of a circular needle may make picking up stitches easier.

Working on the stitches of the lower piece, undo rows to make it shorter or add more rows to make it longer. Then use Kitchener stitch to join the two sections together again.

KNIT KITCHENER STITCH

Lay the pieces to be joined flat, knit side facing you. The sewn stitches will make a knit row.

Bring the needle up through the first stitch of the last row on the lower piece. Go down through the loop at the side edge and up in the center of the next loop on the upper piece, then go down through the first stitch of the lower piece again, and up through the next stitch. Continue until all stitches and loops are joined to make a row.

GARTER KITCHENER STITCH

To keep the pattern correct, make sure that the lower piece of knitting ends with a ridge and the upper piece with a smooth row. To join the pieces, work the lower stitches as for knit Kitchener stitch and the upper stitches as for purl Kitchener stitch.

PURL KITCHENER STITCH

Lay the pieces to be joined flat, purl side facing you. The sewn stitches will make a purl row.

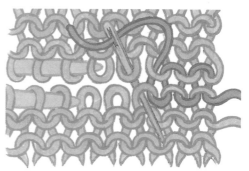

Bring the needle down through the first stitch on the lower piece, up through the loop at the side edge, and down in the center of the next loop on the upper piece. Then go up through the first stitch of the lower piece. Continue in this way along the row, tensioning the sewn stitches as you go.

RIB KITCHENER STITCH

Follow the pattern of the stitches, alternating knit and purl Kitchener stitch. Wide ribs are easier to join than single rib.

EMBROIDERY

EMBROIDERY HAS A GREAT AFFINITY WITH HAND KNITTING. YOU CAN USE THE SAME YARN, A CONTRAST YARN, OR AN EMBROIDERY THREAD. EMBROIDERY DOUBLES THE THICKNESS OF THE FABRIC, SO IT IS BETTER NOT TO USE IT FOR LARGE, SOLID AREAS.

CROSS STITCH ROSE
Cross stitch embroidery works beautifully on stockinette. Each cross stitch covers a single knitted stitch. However, knitted stitches are wider than they are tall, so the cross stitches will not be square. Take this into account when choosing or drawing a chart.

> **Tip**
> *Use a tapestry needle for embroidery and work between the strands of the knitting, rather than splitting the yarn.*

DUPLICATE STITCH
Also known as Swiss darning, this is a clever means of imitating multicolor knitting in stockinette stitch.

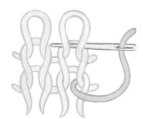

1 Bring the needle out at the base of a stitch. Insert it from right to left under the two strands of the stitch above.

2 Take the needle into the base of the first stitch and out at the base of the next stitch. Continue making each duplicate stitch from right to left, covering knitted stitches.

EYELETS
Single and double eyelets in stockinette can be overcast with matching or contrasting stranded tapestry yarn. Work the eyelets at random or embellish a lace stitch pattern.

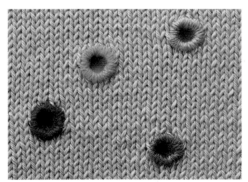

EMBROIDERED EYELETS
Use a single strand of tapestry yarn to make a line of running stitches around the eyelet, then overcast the running stitches and the edge of the eyelet.

CHAIN STITCH
Linear designs are very effective in chain stitch. Instead of working chain stitch with a tapestry needle, try using a medium-to-fine crochet hook—it is easier and faster. Chain stitch can also look very effective worked in the same yarn and color as the stockinette base.

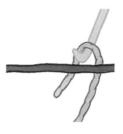

1 Hold the thread underneath the work with your free hand and hold the crochet hook above. Take the hook down through the knitting and pull up a loop of yarn.

2 Insert the hook in the next stitch and pull up a second loop through the first. Continue in this way, working between knitted strands.

CHAIN STITCH MOTIFS
These motifs were made freely with no guidelines. If you want to work a vertical line, perhaps up a rib, skip a strand occasionally to keep the chain lying flat.

CREATING YOUR OWN DESIGNS

Creating a design is simply a matter of common sense, a few calculations—and your imagination.

HOW TO DESIGN

THE WAY IN WHICH YOU APPROACH THE DESIGN PROCESS WILL DEPEND TO A LARGE EXTENT ON PERSONAL PREFERENCE, AND IT MAY EVEN VARY FROM PROJECT TO PROJECT. SOMETIMES IT MAY START WITH AN IDEA FOR A PARTICULAR GARMENT, WHILE AT OTHER TIMES IT MAY START WITH A SWATCH YOU HAVE CREATED.

SEE ALSO

• Sweater design plan, page 51
• Color in design, pages 54–55

The secret of a good design is careful planning. It does not matter if the project is big or small, a blanket or a pair of bootees—the first step is to draw a sketch of what you would like to make. It is surprising how often this will quickly change, but it is always useful to be reminded of your starting point.

Once you are happy with a sketch, look at the drawing and think about the construction of the project. It is useful to draw a diagram or design plan of each piece that will need to be knitted, noting the direction of work and any key measurements. If the project is an item of clothing, the easiest way to ensure that you will achieve the required fit is to measure an existing garment. All measurements made on knitted fabric should be taken with the tape measure held straight along rows or stitches—never around curves. Measure from seam to seam or side to side. Of course, you can also simply take your body measurements and add ease or movement room to suit the style of your design.

Once you have a clear idea of what you would like to make, it is often useful to look through books and magazine, looking not only for similar projects but also details such as buttonbands that you like. Collect all the information together and fill in the detail in your design. Look through the following pages for more tips and advice.

CROSS STITCH CAT
If, even after careful planning, you are not sure how to embellish a project, you can always apply the decoration after the knitting has been completed—and, if you do not like it, you can always unpick it and try something else.

BEADED MITTENS
After you have drawn an initial sketch, sometimes it is easier, and simpler, to find an existing pattern and adapt it to suit your needs. This could be something as simple as embellishing with beads.

SWEATER DESIGN PLAN

WHEN CREATING A DESIGN PLAN FOR A SWEATER, THERE ARE SEVERAL KEY MEASUREMENTS THAT YOU WILL NEED TO HAVE.

SEE ALSO

• How to design, page 50
• Calculating stitches and rows, page 57

The most important measurements are the width and length. Use the diagram below right as a guide to the measurements required.

SLEEVES AND ARMHOLES

The diagram shows only half of the sleeve, so the top edge and cuff edge measurements must be doubled when calculating the width of the sleeve. For a fitted style or a shaped armhole, also record the depth and width of the armhole shaping. There is no need to draw both sleeves unless the sweater is asymmetric and has two different sleeve shapes.

NECKLINES

The neckline is crucial in sweaters because the sweater must fit over the head. This is particularly important when designing for young children—their head to body ratio is quite high. A neckline that is too wide can usually be fixed with an edging.

PRACTICE GOOD DESIGN

It is a good idea to record your design idea by making scale drawings on graph paper. This makes it easier to visualize the final design and will highlight any other measurements that still need to be resolved. It will also be useful if you are calculating the shape of a sleeve top in relation to the depth of an armhole, because the number of stitches and rows in the corresponding edges may vary and must be calculated separately. If you are figuring out unfamiliar shapings, you could make a full-size paper pattern or a toile before you think about calculating stitches and rows.

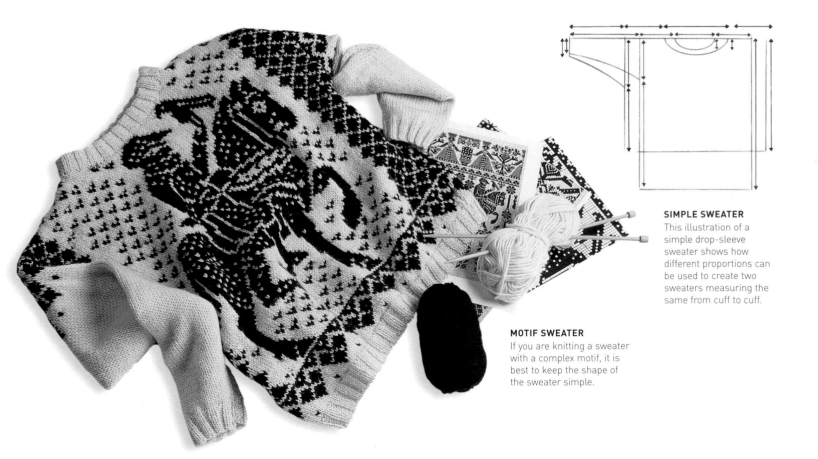

SIMPLE SWEATER
This illustration of a simple drop-sleeve sweater shows how different proportions can be used to create two sweaters measuring the same from cuff to cuff.

MOTIF SWEATER
If you are knitting a sweater with a complex motif, it is best to keep the shape of the sweater simple.

JACKET DESIGN PLAN

THE SAME BASIC PRINCIPLES APPLY FOR DESIGNING A JACKET AS FOR DESIGNING A SWEATER. HOWEVER, THERE ARE A FEW ADDITIONAL FACTORS THAT YOU NEED TO CONSIDER.

FRONT BANDS OR FACINGS

Bands can either be picked up along the front edge of a front piece, or they can be worked separately and sewn to the front edge. However, the smoothest bands are those knitted together with the fronts.

For bands that are knitted with the fronts, choose a stitch pattern with a tighter vertical gauge than that used for the main fabric—for example, garter stitch with a stockinette main fabric. Add the number of band stitches to each front, and change stitch pattern each time you work them. Mark the buttonhole positions on your chart or pattern, and work them in as you

go. For V-neck shaping, decrease in the main stitch pattern next to the band stitches and work the band stitches as before.

REPEAT PATTERNS

Scattered motifs, such as the leaves below, are ideal for cardigans. All you need to do is to plan the size of the back on graph paper, then mark the position of the front edges and the shape of the neck. When placing the motifs—apparently at random—make sure that only whole motifs are on the fronts. To avoid having a band-sized gap on the back, you can make each front exactly half the width of the back.

INTARSIA JACKET
Keep all the design elements together for easy reference.

SEE ALSO
• Sweater design plan, page 51
• Color in design, pages 54–55

Tip
Buy the buttons before you make the buttonholes.

CIRCULAR YOKE DESIGN

THERE IS NO NEED TO FEEL DAUNTED WHEN DESIGNING A CIRCULAR YOKE. TRADITIONAL GARMENT SHAPES DO NOT HAVE TO BE WORKED USING TRADITIONAL TECHNIQUES OR COLORS. AGAIN, THE SAME BASIC PRINCIPLES APPLY AS FOR DESIGNING A SWEATER, WITH SOME ADDITIONAL FACTORS.

CIRCULAR YOKE SWEATER
Each band of pattern will be different, to fit in with the changing stitch counts as the yoke is decreased.

CONSTRUCTION

A yoke garment may be worked from the neck downward with regular increases to create the yoke. At a point just below the underarms, the yoke is divide into two arm sections and two body sections. The front and back body sections are usually joined and work continues downward toward the hem. A yoke garment may also be worked separately from the hem and cuffs upward, then joined and worked in one piece to the neck edge. For the design shown right, the back, front, and sleeves are worked flat before the sections are joined and the yoke is worked in one piece. This method is useful if the lower body has any intarsia work.

PLANNING DECREASES

There are two ways to plan a circular yoke. With narrow bands of pattern, think of the decrease rounds as concentric circles closing in toward the center, and place the decreases on the plain knitted rows between the bands. For large motifs, imagine the yoke as wedge-shaped segments and decrease between the motifs. Space the decreases far apart at the start, then work fewer rounds between decreases to bring the yoke in as you work toward the neck.

SEE ALSO

• Sweater design plan, page 51
• Color in design, pages 54–55

COLOR IN DESIGN

COLOR IS NOT SOMETHING YOU HAVE TO INVENT IF YOU WISH TO DESIGN; IT IS SOMETHING YOU CAN SEE IN THE WORLD AROUND YOU. IF YOU LOVE MULTICOLOR KNITTING, YOU WILL FIND INSPIRATION WHEREVER YOU LOOK.

SEE ALSO

• Texture and color, page 56
• Color knitting, pages 120–121 & 130–131

The color of your project may be the first thing people notice. The color could be the pigments you choose or the light reflected from a texture. It could be the starting point for a design, or it could be inspired by a design idea.

CHARTING COLORS

This can be a useful exercise even if you are not planning a stranded or intarsia knitted project, because it helps to establish the proportions of each color that would suit your design best. If you do not have a charted design in mind, start with a design with a small repeat so that you can see the results of your color experiments quickly. Use colored crayons or pens and start by using two colors in a row, as in classic stranded color knitting, then add more colors or incorporate tiny areas of intarsia. Color more than one repeat to see the effect of this on the color and pattern. Changing the background color and the pattern color each time can produce an interesting flickering stripe. The motifs do not need to be very complicated, because even the simplest patterns come to life if you get the colors right.

CHOOSING YARN COLORS

When you choose yarn colors, do not worry too much about matching them exactly to your inspiration. It is a mistake to be obsessive about matching colors and then forget to consider the fiber content of a yarn. A color may look too bright in the ball, but used in tiny amounts it will wake up the softer shades. Try to think in terms of warm and cool, and light and dark, as well as pigments. Mix in a few yarns with a slight texture to break up the regularity of the surface. Start by knitting your most successful chart design or simply start to knit and change the colors whenever you like.

COLOR INSPIRATION
This little Buddha figure, with its patterned and plain areas, sparks off lots of color combinations for these swatches.

DESIGNING FROM SWATCHES
Knitting swatches can be one of the most satisfying ways to start the design process.

DESIGNING A MOTIF

Simple shapes and bold designs are everywhere, so if you cannot find charted designs you like, be inspired and create your own. It is useful to remember that the more complex the image, the larger the motif will need to be to reproduce the detail, and the simpler the garment shaping should be. To establish your gauge, knit a swatch of part of the chart, then figure out the size of the motif. Although you can use a different yarn, add more background, or frame the motif with another pattern, if you start with a motif design, the size of the motif will dictate the proportions of the garment. Alternatively, you can plan a project and design a motif or series of motifs to fit the project shapes.

Tip

For large motifs, consider working small areas of a particular color using the intarsia technique and the background stranded. Smaller motifs can be worked entirely in stranded knitting.

HOW TO DESIGN A GARMENT WITH MOTIFS

One approach is to establish a stockinette stitch gauge in the yarn you want to use, estimate the size you wish the motif to be, and draw the motif to fit. You may have to make some adjustments to get the best design at a size you can use.

1 Draw the motifs as accurately as you can given the limitations of graph paper, which makes drawing curves difficult. As you draw, think about the techniques you will use.

3 Once you have designed the motif, draw a full-size chart for the back of the garment, photocopy the motif several times, then cut out the motifs and move them around on the large chart until you have the desired effect.

2 Knit swatches of each design element. Adjust the shapes and experiment with color knitting techniques until you knit a swatch that you like.

ADAPTING A CROSS STITCH CHART

Keen color knitters are often tempted to knit from cross stitch charts. They are a particularly rich source of type designs. If you decide to adapt a cross stitch chart, remember that each cross stitch on fabric is square, whereas each knitted stitch is a wide and short V shape. With the stranded color knitting technique, you may have an almost square gauge that does not distort the design too much. However, if you use the intarsia technique to knit directly from a cross stitch chart, the design will be compressed vertically.

KELIM TEXTILES

Old textiles translate particularly well into knitted fabrics. Make a color fringe to keep with the chart for easy yarn reference.

Tip

For organic shapes such as flowers, try designing subtle variations instead of working identical motifs.

TEXTURE AND COLOR

COLOR IS NOT ONLY CREATED BY PIGMENT, BUT ALSO BY THE EFFECT OF LIGHT ON A TEXTURE. ONE THING KNITTED FABRIC HAS IN ABUNDANCE IS TEXTURE—IT MAY BE THE SIMPLE TEXTURE OF THE STITCH, THE TEXTURE OF THE YARN, OR THE RAISED TEXTURE OF BOBBLES AND CABLES.

COMBINING TEXTURED PATTERNS

Creating a design with textured stitch patterns is just like planning any other repeat pattern— all you have to do is use the gauge to figure out the measurements. The only difference is that, if you are combining cables with another stitch pattern or putting different cables together, you will need to take the gauge of each cable panel and stitch pattern separately. Calculate the size of each panel, then add them together to establish the width. To adjust the design to get the measurement you want, change the number of stitches between panels. If designing a jacket or cardigan, make sure that only whole panels are on the fronts. If the back is to mirror the front pieces, make each front exactly half the width of the back to avoid having a band-sized gap on the back.

EXPERIMENTING WITH CABLES

Cable panels can be very effective used as an accent to your design. Here, they frame rows of heart motifs with moss stitch at each side.

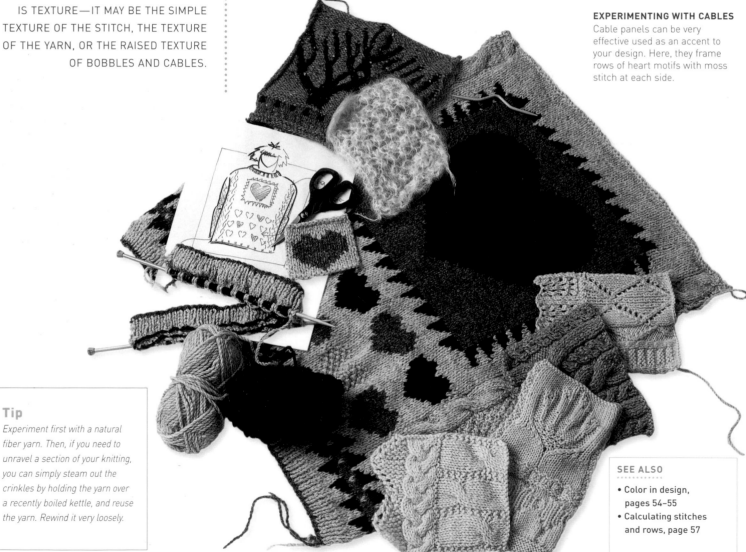

Tip

Experiment first with a natural fiber yarn. Then, if you need to unravel a section of your knitting, you can simply steam out the crinkles by holding the yarn over a recently boiled kettle, and reuse the yarn. Rewind it very loosely.

SEE ALSO

• Color in design, pages 54–55
• Calculating stitches and rows, page 57

CALCULATING STITCHES AND ROWS

ONCE YOU HAVE FINISHED YOUR DESIGN PLAN, YOU WILL NEED TWO SETS OF MEASUREMENTS TO TRANSLATE YOUR DESIGN INTO STITCHES AND ROWS—THE SIZE OF YOUR STITCHES AND THE SIZE OF YOUR PROJECT.

SEE ALSO
• How to design, page 50
• Sweater design plan, page 51

First, find out the size of your stitches. To do this, write down the gauge of the swatch as so many stitches and so many rows to 4in (10cm). This will be more accurate than measuring a smaller unit such as 1in or 1cm. Ensure that you have a diagram of each piece to be worked in the project, with measurements.

NUMBER CRUNCHING
To translate the measurements into stitches and rows, use a calculator for speed and accuracy. Here, measurements are given in inches and centimeters, but always work in one or the other—do not mix them. For example, if your gauge is 22 stitches to 4in (10cm), divide the stitches by 4 (10) to give 5.5 stitches per inch (2.2 stitches per cm).

To calculate how many stitches to cast on for a width of 24 inches with a gauge of 5.5 stitches to one inch?
5.5 multiplied by 24 = 132 stitches

To calculate how many stitches to cast on for a width of 61 centimeters with a gauge of 2.2 stitches to one centimeter?
2.2 multiplied by 61 = 134 stitches

Calculate the number of rows in the same way, using the row gauge.

PLANNING REPEATS
If you are using stockinette stitch, you can cast on the precise number of stitches needed for the width (plus two stitches that will be lost in the side seams when they are sewn up). Add or subtract a stitch or two to balance a ribbed edge. If you are using a textured stitch pattern, you will have to calculate how many multiples of the pattern—plus any edge stitches—come closest to fitting into your measurements. Check the row repeats in relation to the length in the same way.

Stockinette can be worked on any number of rows, but if working in a textured stitch, you may want to shape the shoulder or neck at the end of a pattern repeat or on a specific pattern row to avoid an ugly break. It is sometimes useful to draw your final design again on knitter's graph paper that matches your gauge, allowing one stitch to each square. Adapt measurements or stitch patterns until you are happy with the proportions of your design. You are now as well prepared as you can be and are finally ready to start knitting the project.

PLAN YOUR GARMENT
Plan a project in as much detail as you can and keep the diagrams, swatches, and samples together.

CHAPTER TWO

Stitch Collection

This chapter features design ideas and inspiration themed by stitch style. The introductory pages for each style discuss key aspects of the techniques involved, followed by a number of carefully selected stitch patterns to inform and inspire you further.

KNIT AND PURL

KNIT AND PURL STITCH PATTERNS CAN BE USED TO CREATE ANYTHING FROM PILLOWS AND TRADITIONAL SWEATERS TO FASHION DESIGNS IN CRUNCHY TEXTURES AND SUBTLE BROCADES—THE POSSIBILITIES ARE ENDLESS.

SEE ALSO
....
• Knit and purl stitch patterns, pages 62–69

Alternate knit and purl and you get the simplest texture stitches. Group the knits and purls geometrically to make blocks, diagonals, chevrons, and diamonds, or put them together more freely to create motifs. Patterns can be repeated to make an allover design, or used in panels with simple stitch patterns between.

On a practical level, a mixture of knit and purl stitches on a row or up a column of stitches creates a flatter fabric—one less prone to the curling of stockinette stitch or the contracting of many rib stitch patterns. This characteristic is often used in edging stitch patterns and for collars and facings.

PUTTING KNIT AND PURL TOGETHER
On the right side of the fabric, the knit stitches appear smooth, while each purl stitch makes a little blip. If you think of the smooth stitches as light and the blips as dark, you will find it easy to read the charts on the following pages.

WORKING INTO THE BACK OF A STITCH
Working into the back of stitches is often used to add definition to a stitch pattern. It closes up the V shape on the right side of the fabric and makes the diagonals from bottom right to top left more prominent. As the knitting progresses, these diagonals emphasize the verticals on the right side of the fabric.

TO KNIT INTO THE BACK OF A STITCH
Insert the right needle into the back of the stitch from right to left, take the yarn around the needle, and make the new stitch in the usual way.

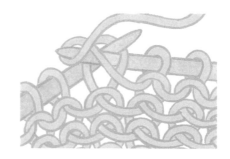

TO PURL INTO THE BACK OF A STITCH
Swing the needle ends slightly away from you to insert the right needle into the back of the stitch from left to right, then take the yarn around the needle and make a new stitch in the usual way.

SEED STITCH
With an odd number of stitches, seed stitch is a one-row pattern. On every row, simply knit the first stitch, then purl one, knit one to the end of the row. On an even number of stitches, seed stitch is a two-row pattern (see page 62 for chart).

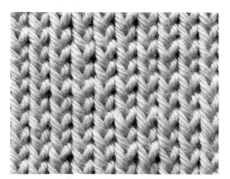

CROSSED STOCKINETTE
To work crossed stockinette stitch, knit into the back of each stitch on right-side rows and purl into the back of each stitch on wrong-side rows.

SLIPPING A STITCH

To slip a stitch, simply move it from the left to the right needle without working it. When this is done as part of a stitch pattern, the stitch is usually slipped purlwise, so that the stitch lies on the needle in the same direction as an ordinary knit stitch.

Slipping stitches makes a close, firm fabric. If the stitch is slipped purlwise on a right-side row with the yarn at the back, the design element is vertical. If the stitch is slipped purlwise on a right-side row with the yarn at the front, the design element is horizontal.

Stitches can also be slipped purlwise on wrong-side rows. If the yarn is held in front, the strand will not show on the right side; if the yarn is held at the back, the strand will show on the right side.

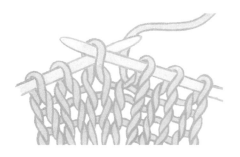

TO SLIP ONE STITCH WITH THE YARN AT THE BACK ON A KNIT ROW

Insert the right needle into the stitch as if to purl, then slip the stitch from the left to the right needle. Do not take the yarn around the needle—there is no new stitch.

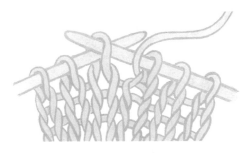

TO SLIP ONE STITCH WITH THE YARN AT THE FRONT ON A KNIT ROW

Bring the yarn to the front, insert the right needle into the stitch as if to purl, then slip the stitch from the left to the right needle. Take the yarn to the back of the work to knit the next stitch.

BARRED STOCKINETTE
Purl on wrong-side rows; on right-side rows, knit and, holding the yarn in front, slip alternate stitches.

GUERNSEY SWEATERS

For further inspiration, look at the traditional fisherman's sweaters known as Guernseys or Ganseys, from the British island of Guernsey. Using yarn that has a firm twist, these sweaters are knitted in a tight gauge and predominately knit and purl stitch patterns, which become particularly well defined when knitted in a firm gauge.

SIMPLE SWEATER
A combination of knit and purl stitches makes this richly textured design.

Seed stitch

MULTIPLE OF 2 STITCHES PLUS 1

MULTIPLE OF 2 STITCHES PLUS 2

Over an odd number of stitches, you can start seed stitch with either a knit or a purl stitch. Over an even number of stitches, if the first stitch of the first row is knit, the first stitch of the second row will be purl.

Little blocks

MULTIPLE OF 6 STITCHES PLUS 3

Patterns of alternating blocks of stockinette stitch and reverse stockinette stitch can be worked over any combination of stitches and rows. Block patterns have a similar gauge to that of stockinette stitch, so the little blocks here appear square even though there are more rows than stitches to each block.

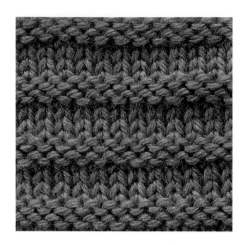

Welting

MULTIPLE OF ANY NUMBER OF STITCHES

Welting patterns can be worked on any number of stitches, odd or even, and with any combination of rows of reverse stockinette stitch and stockinette stitch. This fabric spreads widthwise and contracts vertically.

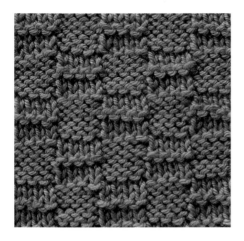

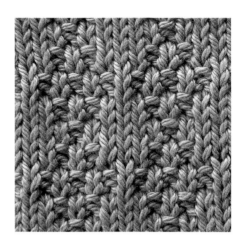

Broken blocks

MULTIPLE OF 8 STITCHES PLUS 10

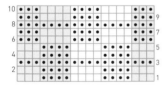

Adding a garter ridge to the stockinette stitch blocks makes this pattern look more exciting than plain blocks, yet it is very easy to work.

Moss stitch

MULTIPLE OF 2 STITCHES PLUS 1

Moss stitch is extremely useful because the row gauge is similar to that of stockinette stitch, which makes it ideal for creating textured motifs on a stockinette stitch background (see moss stitch star and heart on page 66). The chart shows moss stitch beginning with purl, because this holds the corner of the knitting more neatly. If moss stitch is to be used after p1, k1 rib, then start with a knit stitch, as in the third row of the chart.

Tiny moss diamonds

MULTIPLE OF 6 STITCHES PLUS 1

This stitch shows the smallest possible moss stitch diamonds on stockinette stitch. Use it as an allover pattern, or work just three or four repeats for a textured panel.

KEY TO CHART SYMBOLS pages 140–141

Cornish lattice

MULTIPLE OF 6 STITCHES PLUS 3

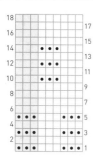

This stitch pattern is based on purl garter stitch and stockinette, which makes it easy to work.

Garter diamonds

MULTIPLE OF 20 STITCHES PLUS 1

Although the large repeat makes this pattern look complicated, it is easy to work because it is made with knit and purl stitches on right-side rows, and every wrong-side row is just purl.

Twisted little check

MULTIPLE OF 10 STITCHES PLUS 1

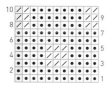

Working the stockinette stitch squares through the back of the loops gives a lovely definition to the blocks.

Twisted diagonal

MULTIPLE OF 8 STITCHES PLUS 2

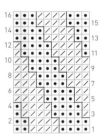

You could work the stockinette stitch part of this pattern without twisting the stitches, but the result would be less well-defined diagonals. For a diagonal running to the right, reverse the chart.

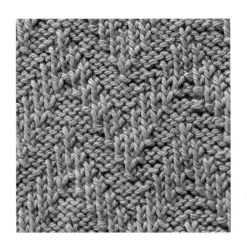

Twisted chevron

MULTIPLE OF 12 STITCHES PLUS 1

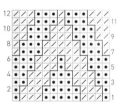

When diagonals are worked in alternate directions, they meet to make chevrons. Working stitches through the back of the loops makes the chevrons appear taller and more elegant.

Twisted square check

MULTIPLE OF 10 STITCHES PLUS 2

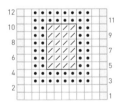

See how the small blocks of stitches, which are worked through the back of the loops, contrast with the stockinette stitch outlining the blocks.

KEY TO CHART SYMBOLS pages 140–141

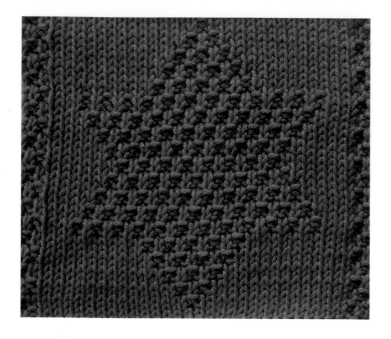

Moss stitch star

MOTIF OF 23 STITCHES

This star can be used as a single motif, scattered on a stockinette stitch background, or repeated in blocks. If you are planning to use it as a repeat pattern, chart it out in full to make sure that you have allowed enough extra stockinette background stitches between the stars.

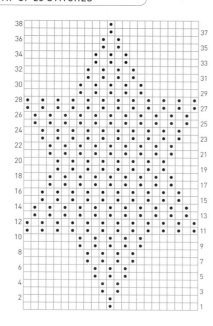

Moss stitch heart

MOTIF OF 25 STITCHES

This heart motif can be used in the same way as the moss stitch star (left) or combined with other stitch patterns. It is very easy to make this motif larger—simply copy the design onto graph paper, then add more pairs of dots for purl stitches evenly all around the motif until the heart is the size you want.

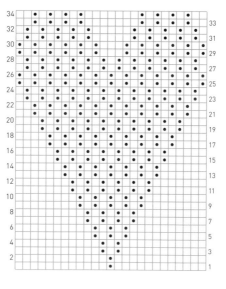

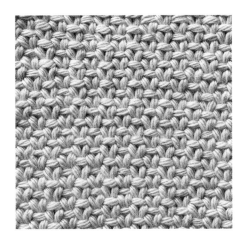

Linen stitch

MULTIPLE OF 2 STITCHES PLUS 3

This densely woven fabric is made by slipping stitches on both right- and wrong-side rows. Remember to bring the yarn forward before slipping a stitch on right-side rows, and to take the yarn back before slipping a stitch on wrong-side rows, so that the strands always appear on the right side of the work.

Slip stitch herringbone

MULTIPLE OF 8 STITCHES PLUS 7

Slipping two stitches creates the horizontal strands in this subtle pattern. When you are slipping two stitches, it is easier to slip them purlwise together. Do not strand too tightly, because it will pull in and make a very thick fabric.

Butterfly blocks

MULTIPLE OF 10 STITCHES PLUS 7

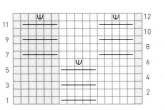

Ⓤ   Take right needle under the three long strands and knit them with the stitch.

Stranded fabrics are not all heavy. In this pattern, also called bowknot, the long strands are linked into a knit stitch to make a lively variation on simple blocks.

KEY TO CHART SYMBOLS pages 140–141

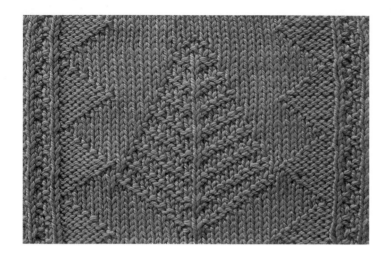

Tree and flags

MULTIPLE OF 40 STITCHES PLUS 1

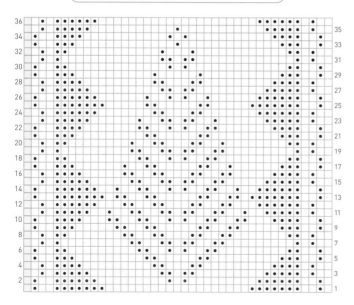

Note the way the flag panels just miss touching the tree. The busy little pattern between the flag panels is simply moss stitch.

Hearts and chevrons

PANEL OF 5 STITCHES / 11 STITCHES / 5 STITCHES / 15 STITCHES

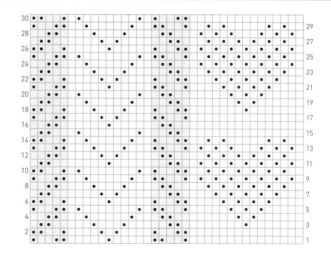

These diagonal, chevron, and heart patterns can all be used as separate panels. The chevron panel is a 10-row repeat, so it fits neatly into the 30-row repeat of the heart panel. The tiny diagonals repeat every 4 rows, so you will need to work 60 rows before the pattern repeats exactly.

Diamond and net

(MULTIPLE OF 42 STITCHES PLUS 3)

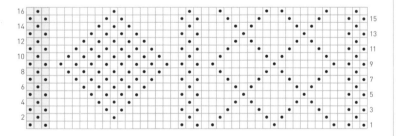

The seed stitch diamond is so satisfying because its shape echoes the diamond contained in the crisscross of the net.

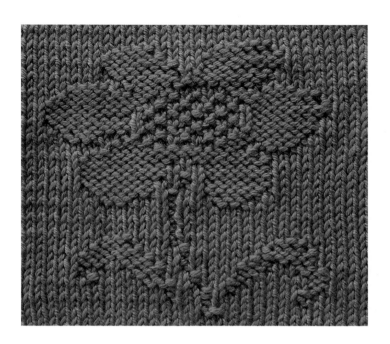

Daisy

(MOTIF OF 25 STITCHES)

Knit and purl stitches can be used to draw naturalistic motifs, using the play of light on the surface of the knitting to define the design. If you want a daisy leaning in the opposite direction, copy the chart onto graph paper in reverse. For a smooth-petaled daisy on a textured background, all you have to do is reverse the knit and purl stitches.

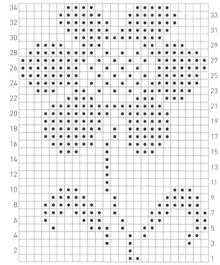

KEY TO CHART SYMBOLS pages 140–141

RIB

SIMPLE RIBS ARE COMBINATIONS OF KNIT AND PURL STITCHES THAT FORM VERTICALS AND CONTRACT THE KNITTING ACROSS THE WIDTH.

In rib, the knit stitches are raised and the purl stitches sink down. The resulting elasticity makes rib very suitable for edgings and cuffs. Some ribbed garments are designed to fit closely, but choice of yarn is important. Wool, for example, will make a springy, stretchy rib, while cotton ribs will lie flat. In the wrong yarn, a skinny rib sweater just will not cling.

Ribs are usually worked on needles one, two, or more sizes smaller than for other stitches.

The smaller the needle size, the more the rib will contract. Interesting patterns can be made by combining simple rib with cable, lace, and twist stitches.

Measuring the length of a piece of ribbing can be difficult, because this measurement will vary depending on whether the knitting is stretched or contracted widthwise. In the end, it is best to measure ribs half-stretched unless the instructions state otherwise.

POPULAR RIB PATTERNS

There are some rib patterns whose versatility and durability make them a popular choice.

SINGLE RIB

For this basic rib, alternate knit and purl stitches are worked above each other.

Over an even number of stitches: Repeat k1, p1 to the end of the of each row.

Over an odd number of stitches: Begin k1, then repeat p1, k1 to the end. On alternate rows begin p1, then k1, p1 to the end.

BAGGY RIB STITCHES

In rib patterns, the knit stitch that immediately precedes a purl stitch is often a bit larger than the others. One solution is to work this knit stitch slightly more firmly. Another option is to knit into the back of this knit stitch, then wrap the yarn clockwise around the needle rather than counterclockwise when working the following purl stitch.

SEE ALSO
• Rib stitch patterns, pages 72–79

DOUBLE RIB

Knit two, purl two rib makes a very elastic fabric with strongly defined ridges and furrows.

Working double rib

This rib can be worked on a number of stitches divisible by four, in which case k2, p2 is repeated along each row. To balance it at each end, work on a number of stitches divisible by four, plus two. The first row begins k2 and is followed by p2, k2 repeated to the end. The second row begins p2, followed by k2, p2 to the end.

BROKEN DOUBLE RIB

This variation on double rib does not pull in. The right side of the fabric is worked as a double rib and on the purl side all the stitches are purled.

RIB VARIATIONS

There are several more stitch patterns that, at first glance, have the appearance of one of the more popular ribs but are in fact more than just a combination of knit and purl stitches.

FISHERMAN'S RIB

Fisherman's rib is an interesting variation on single rib. Knitting alternate stitches in the row below gives a deeper, softer rib. It is often confused with brioche rib, which is slightly loftier.

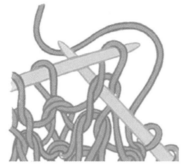

BRIOCHE RIB

Brioche rib is made with slip stitches and yarn overs; there are no purl stitches. Instructions are charted on page 79.

Working brioche rib
When knitting together a slip stitch and a yarn over, the two strands are already in place on the needle and are knitted together in the usual way.

Working fisherman's rib
The stitch is knitted in the usual way, except that the point of the right needle goes into the stitch directly underneath the first stitch on the left needle. Both strands are then dropped off the needle together.

RIB YOKE

The yoke of this child's cardigan is worked in a series of offset rib patterns. The elastic rib ensures a perfect fit and the purl troughs are an excellent place to discreetly work the increases.

Single rib

MULTIPLE OF 2 STITCHES PLUS 1

Alternate knit and purl stitches make up
this rib. It is also called knit one, purl one
rib or one-and-one rib.

Broken single rib

MULTIPLE OF 2 STITCHES PLUS 1

Purling the wrong-side rows reduces the
elasticity of the rib and produces an
attractive texture.

Twisted single rib

MULTIPLE OF 2 STITCHES PLUS 1

This well-defined rib has the knit stitches
on the right side and the purl stitches on
the wrong side worked through the back
of the loops.

Double rib

MULTIPLE OF 4 STITCHES PLUS 2

Also known as knit two, purl two rib or two-and-two rib, this classic stitch is the same on both sides.

Broken double rib

MULTIPLE OF 4 STITCHES PLUS 2

Purling wrong-side rows turns classic double rib into a firm fabric with verticals of stockinette stitch and garter stitch.

Bamboo rib

MULTIPLE OF 8 STITCHES PLUS 6

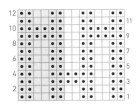

Interspersing the double rib pattern with small bands of welting makes an interesting variation on a familiar theme.

KEY TO CHART SYMBOLS pages 140–141

Diagonal double rib

MULTIPLE OF 4 STITCHES

Moving the double rib pattern along one stitch on alternate rows produces well-defined diagonals.

Wide rib

MULTIPLE OF 8 STITCHES PLUS 2

A wide rib can comprise any number of stitches. This one combines six of stockinette stitch with two of reverse stockinette stitch.

Welted rib

MULTIPLE OF 6 STITCHES

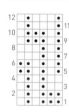

Joining up single ribs with small blocks of welting makes an allover diagonal pattern.

Shadow rib

MULTIPLE OF 3 STITCHES PLUS 2

Knitting a stitch through the back of the loop on right-side rows creates a neat little blip on a reverse stockinette stitch ground.

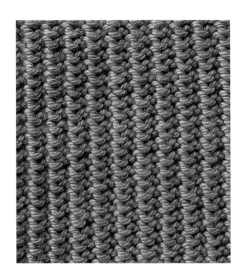

Close stitch

MULTIPLE OF 2 STITCHES PLUS 1

Slipped stitches make this gentle rib very thick and soft—ideal for socks.

Crossed rib

MULTIPLE OF 3 STITCHES PLUS 1

⊻— Sl 1 knitwise, k in front and back of next st, pass sl st over.

Although it looks like a twisted rib, this effect is achieved by passing a slipped stitch over an increase.

KEY TO CHART SYMBOLS pages 140–141

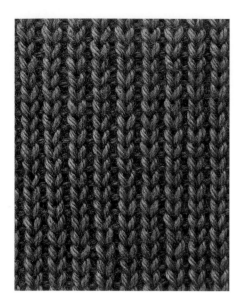

Stocking heel rib

MULTIPLE OF 2 STITCHES PLUS 1

This stitch pattern is used to reinforce sock and stocking heels.

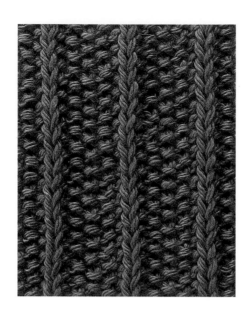

Seed and slip stitch rib

MULTIPLE OF 6 STITCHES PLUS 5

Seed stitch panels make this slip stitch rib extra firm and substantial.

Cartridge belt rib

MULTIPLE OF 4 STITCHES PLUS 3

Slipping stitches on both sides of the knitting gives well-defined ridges and a fabric that is the same on both sides.

Seed rib

MULTIPLE OF 6 STITCHES PLUS 1

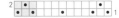

Another reversible stitch, this combines single rib and seed stitch.

Broken seed rib

MULTIPLE OF 10 STITCHES PLUS 3

Dividing stockinette stitch panels with seed stitch gives a flat, mock rib.

Embossed rib

MULTIPLE OF 4 STITCHES PLUS 3

This firm rib combines stitches worked through the back of the loops with a nubbly knit and purl texture.

KEY TO CHART SYMBOLS pages 140–141

Moss rib

MULTIPLE OF 6 STITCHES PLUS 1

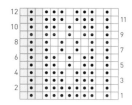

Panels of moss stitch alternate with single rib.

Moss diamond rib

MULTIPLE OF 10 STITCHES PLUS 3

Both sides of this rib are attractive. On the reverse, the diamonds sit on a stockinette stitch background and the ribs are less conspicuous.

Fisherman's rib

MULTIPLE OF 2 STITCHES PLUS 3

Ⅴ K in row below.

Knitting alternate stitches in the row below is the secret of this deep, soft rib. Both sides look the same. After working row 1, repeat only rows 2 and 3.

Brioche rib

MULTIPLE OF 2 STITCHES PLUS 3

⊖ Yfwd, sl 1 purlwise, take yarn
    over needle.

△ K tog the sl st and yo.

This rib looks similar to fisherman's rib but
is made quite differently.

Tilted rib

MULTIPLE OF 42 STITCHES PLUS 8

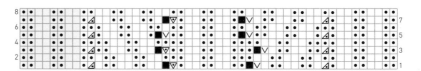

Panels of diagonal ribs are made
with increases and decreases.

▽ Purl into front of stitch,
    then k into back of stitch.

KEY TO CHART SYMBOLS pages 140–141

CABLES

KNITTING GROUPS OF STITCHES OUT OF SEQUENCE CREATES SOME OF THE WORLD'S MOST EXCITING STITCH PATTERNS. CABLES CAN BE WORKED WITH TWO OR MORE STITCHES, AND THEY CAN BE CROSSED TO THE FRONT OR THE BACK TO MAKE HUNDREDS OF COILING AND INTERLACING STITCH PATTERNS.

SEE ALSO

• Texture and color, page 56
• Cable stitch patterns, pages 82–89

Cable stitches are most commonly associated with Aran sweaters, the traditional fisherman's sweaters from the Aran Islands off the coast of Ireland, in which panels of ropes, braids, diamonds, trellis, and embossed stitches are combined to flamboyant effect. Modern knit designers often combine cable stitches to make fascinating figurative motifs. Classic cables are more restrained and give a sophisticated touch to the plainest garment.

HOW TO CABLE

Cabling involves transferring one, two, or more stitches onto a short double-pointed needle. When the cable needle is held at the back, the stitches on the right side of the work make a diagonal from left to right. When the cable needle is held at the front, the stitches make a diagonal from right to left. Cable stitches can be knitted, purled, or textured as directed in the pattern instructions.

Once you have mastered the techniques for basic four-stitch cables shown here, you will be able to tackle any cable stitch pattern. You will also find it easy to customize cables, such as making them wider or taller, or cabling more frequently for a firmer fabric or less often for a softer effect.

BACK CABLE
This four-stitch cable crosses at the back and all the stitches are knitted.

1 Slip the first two stitches onto a cable needle and hold at the back of the work, then knit the next two stitches from the left needle.

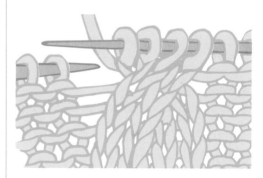

2 Knit the two stitches from the cable needle.

CABLE SWEATER
Simple cables at each side of a bold center panel make a chunky sweater.

FRONT CABLE
All the stitches are knitted, but this four-stitch cable crosses at the front.

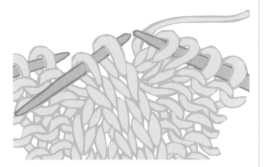

1 Slip the first two stitches onto a cable needle and hold at the front of the work, then knit the next two stitches from the left needle.

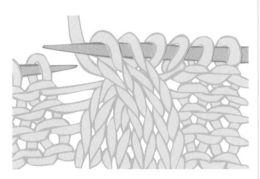

2 Knit the two stitches from the cable needle.

BACK PURL CABLE
This four-stitch cable has knit stitches making a diagonal to the right on a purl background.

1 Slip the first two stitches onto a cable needle and hold at the back of the work, then knit the next two stitches from the left needle.

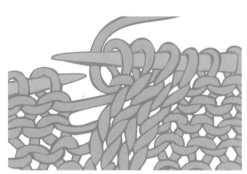

2 Purl the two stitches from the cable needle.

FRONT PURL CABLE
This four-stitch cable has knit stitches making a diagonal to the left on a purl background.

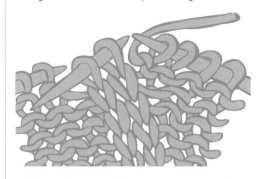

1 Slip the first two stitches onto a cable needle and hold at the front of the work, then purl the next two stitches from the left needle.

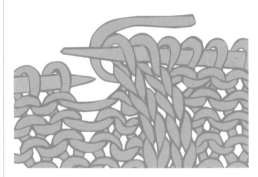

2 Knit the two stitches from the cable needle.

ROPES AND WAVES
On the center two columns of stitches, front and back cables are repeated to make ropes, while at each side they are alternated to make waves.

HONEYCOMB AND ZIGZAG
Knit and purl four-stitch cables are used to make these patterns.

Tip
Counting rows between cables can be tricky. Slip a marker of contrast yarn between stitches on the cable row and pull it out afterward.

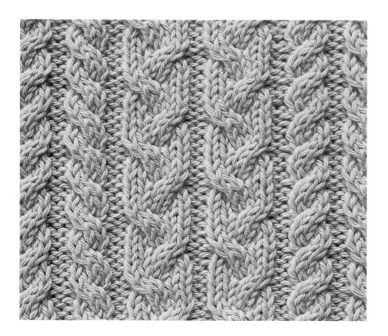

Braids and ropes

MULTIPLE OF 28 STITCHES

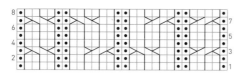

Little cables worked over four rows are fine on their own, but are especially good for slipping in between bigger panels. Here, they are used with eight-row braids.

Four-strand braid and snake cables

PANEL OF 44 STITCHES

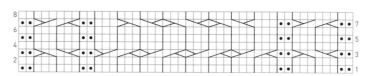

This panel is surprisingly easy to work, because all the wrong-side rows are just purl. There is no limit to the number of strands you can braid—just add six more stitches for each strand.

Oxo and honeycomb

PANEL OF 44 STITCHES

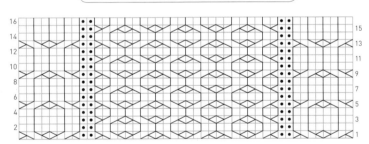

The center panel of honeycomb cable has a repeat of eight stitches, so you could work it over any multiple of eight to make it wider or narrower.

Cable check

MULTIPLE OF 12 STITCHES PLUS 6

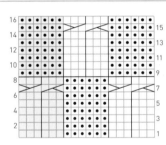

The three-over-three cables at the top of each block make this simple pattern of knit and purl blocks look more complicated than it really is.

KEY TO CHART SYMBOLS **pages 140–141**

Little cable ribs

MULTIPLE OF 13 STITCHES PLUS 6

Twists are often used to make two-stitch crosses, but the smooth effect created by true cabling is worth the extra work, as this pattern shows. You could make the spiral rib wider by adding any multiple of two stitches.

Triple zigzag and rope

PANEL OF 36 STITCHES

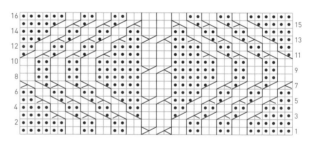

This zigzag is the same as the one on page 81, but it looks a lot more interesting in a group of three rather than two. Reverse the rope cable if you are working a pair of panels.

Cable knot rib

MULTIPLE OF 14 STITCHES PLUS 8

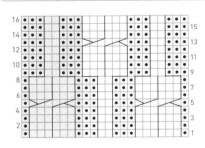

This six-stitch cable alternates with a two-stitch rib. The pattern looks very busy, but it is easy to do.

Braid and rib

MULTIPLE OF 12 STITCHES PLUS 3

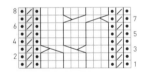

If you would like a fatter braid, try working over twelve stitches, cabling four over four each time.

Deckle edge

MULTIPLE OF 12 STITCHES PLUS 2

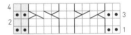

Two-over-two cables along the edges of stockinette stitch panels contrast effectively with narrow bands of garter stitch. All wrong-side rows are purled.

KEY TO CHART SYMBOLS pages 140–141

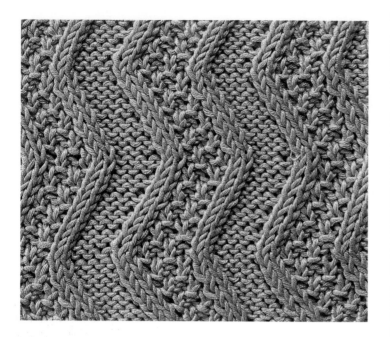

Two-texture zigzag

MULTIPLE OF 14 STITCHES PLUS 2

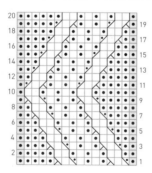

This pattern is a good one for getting used to knit and purl cables, because the purl stitch always fits into the moss stitch. To reverse the zigzag, start the chart on row 11.

Smocked cable

PANEL OF 24 STITCHES

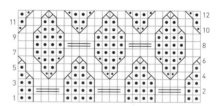

K4, sl all 4 sts onto cable needle and hold at front. Wind yarn tightly counterclockwise around sts on cable needle 4 times, ending at wrong side. Sl 4 sts back onto right needle.

Although smocking can be created by sewing ribs together, using cables and clusters gives better definition. This technique can be used to simulate other popular smocking designs.

Textured cable

MULTIPLE OF 16 STITCHES PLUS 10

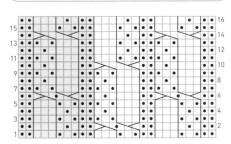

 Sl 3 sts onto cable needle and hold at front, k3, then k1, p1, k1 from cable needle.

Sl 3 sts onto cable needle and hold at front, k1, p1, k1, then k3 from cable needle.

Single rib could be substituted, with the knit stitches worked through the back of the loops.

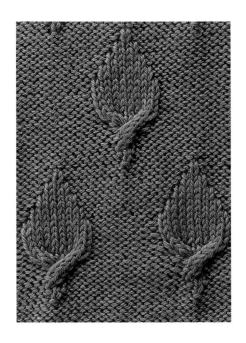

Leaf cable

MULTIPLE OF 18 STITCHES PLUS 9

These cabled leaves are used here for an allover pattern, but they could also be combined with other cable stitches.

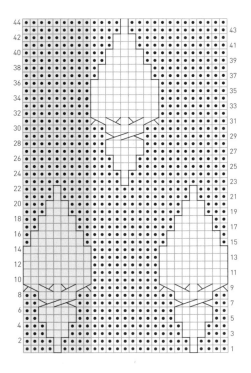

Ribbed cable

PANEL OF 12 STITCHES

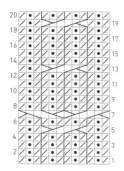 Sl 3 sts onto cable needle and hold at back. K1 tbl, p1, k1 tbl, then k1 tbl, p1, k1 tbl from cable needle.

As above, but hold cable needle at front.

Crossed stitches are worked with this ribbed cable.

Tulip cable

PANEL OF 10 STITCHES

All k sts of cables are worked tbl.

One-over-one cables and stitches crossed by working through the back of the loops form stylized flowers.

Ovals and flowers

PANEL OF 34 STITCHES

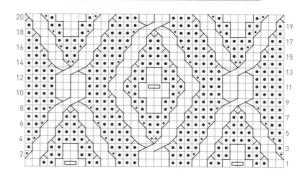 K2, sl these 2 sts onto cable needle and hold at front. Wind yarn counterclockwise around sts on cable needle 3 times, ending at wrong side. Sl 2 sts back onto right needle.

Cabling on wrong-side rows is no harder than cabling on the right side, and because the stitches from the four-stitch cable are cabled again on the next row, they spring out cleanly.

Horseshoe trellis

MULTIPLE OF 16 STITCHES PLUS 2

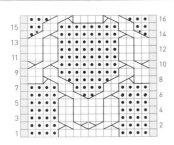

Extra cables springing out of the background add interest to an allover trellis pattern.

PANEL OF 21 STITCHES

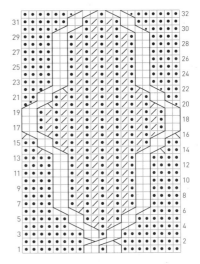

Sl 2 sts onto cable needle and hold at back, k2, then p1, k1 tbl from cable needle.

Sl 2 sts onto cable needle and hold at front, k1 tbl, p1, then k2 from cable needle.

Brocade

Elegant curves can be made with very simple cables. This stitch pattern can be used as a panel, or staggered as a repeat.

TWISTS

TWISTS INVOLVE WORKING TWO OR THREE STITCHES OUT OF SEQUENCE, BUT WITHOUT USING A CABLE NEEDLE. THIS IS AN EASY WAY TO CREATE PATTERNS WHERE LINES OF STITCHES TRAVEL OVER THE SURFACE OF THE KNITTING.

Some twist stitch patterns look like miniature cables, while others create diagonals, zigzags, and diamonds. Twisting stitches closes up the work, so densely twisted stitched patterns can make the fabric thicker and less flexible—unless larger needles are used.

Twists are sometimes combined with cables, with the shallower twists complementing the depths of the cables. The advantage of twist stitches is that they can be worked more quickly than cable stitches.

Although twists are easy to do, there are lots of tiny but important variations that change the appearance of a twist. They can be worked on right- or wrong-side rows, and the stitches can be all knit, all purl, or a combination of the two.

Twist stitch patterns are easy to work in the round from a chart, especially patterns that move a stitch on every row. Simply read every row of the chart from right to left, interpreting all the symbols as right-side row twists.

HOW TO WORK A LEFT TWIST
In this right-side row twist, the first stitch on the left needle lies on top and slants to the left, while the second stitch lies behind and is worked first through the back of the loop.

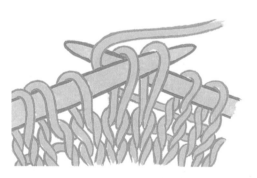

1 Knit into the back of the second stitch.

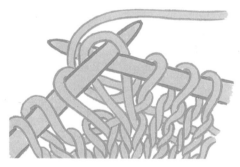

2 Knit into the front of the first stitch.

3 Slip both stitches off the left needle together.

SEE ALSO
• Texture and color, page 56
• Twist stitch patterns, pages 92–99

LEFT TWIST VARIATIONS
To work a knit and purl two-stitch twist slanting to the left, purl into the back of the second stitch, then knit into the front of the first stitch.

To twist two stitches to the left on a wrong-side row, purl into the back of the second stitch, then purl into the front of the first stitch.

HERRINGBONE TWIST

This twist pattern uses left and right twists on a stockinette stitch background, but the top stitches of the twists are made more prominent by slipping them on wrong-side rows.

HOW TO WORK A RIGHT TWIST

In this right-side row twist, the second stitch on the left needle lies on top and slants to the right, while the first stitch lies behind and is worked through the back of the loop.

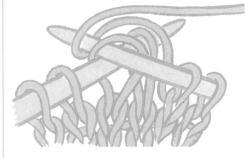

1 Knit into the front of the second stitch.

2 Knit into the back of the first stitch.

3 Slip both stitches off the left needle together.

TWIST STITCH SWEATER

A stonewash effect gives this cotton sweater with a twist stitch diamond pattern an extra dimension.

RIGHT TWIST VARIATIONS

There are two other ways of working the knit twist shown above. Either knit into the front instead of the back of the first stitch in step 2; or knit two together, then knit the first stitch again before slipping the stitches off the left needle.

To work a knit and purl right twist, knit into the front of the second stitch, then purl into the front the first stitch.

To twist two stitches to the right on a wrong-side row, purl into the front of the second stitch, then purl into the front of the first stitch.

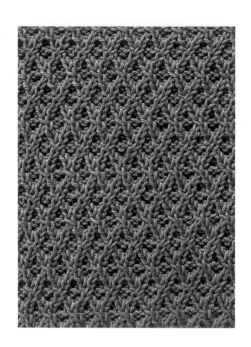

Herringbone twist

MULTIPLE OF 6 STITCHES PLUS 3

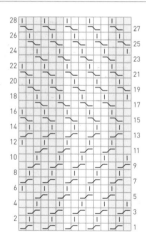

This pattern is often used as a side panel on garments or even socks.

Tiny trellis

MULTIPLE OF 4 STITCHES PLUS 2

If worked over 10 stitches, this pattern makes a crossed diamond panel.

Miniature braid

MULTIPLE OF 4 STITCHES PLUS 1

Use this pattern as an interesting alternative to rib; simply plan more purl stitches between braids to suit your design.

Branched rib

MULTIPLE OF 16 STITCHES PLUS 2

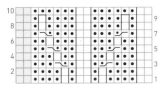

This decorated rib does not pull in very much, so it can be used as an allover pattern. If you want all the branches to twist in the same direction, repeat the first or last eight stitches of the chart.

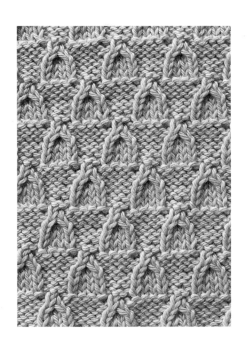

Bellflower blocks

MULTIPLE OF 8 STITCHES PLUS 6

Simply twisting the stitches at the top of each block produces this pretty pattern. See the bellflower motif on page 99 for another use of these blocks.

Slip stitch ovals

MULTIPLE OF 12 STITCHES PLUS 8

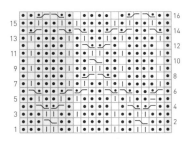

Slipping stitches on wrong-side rows beneath the twist gives a graceful curve to oval mock cables.

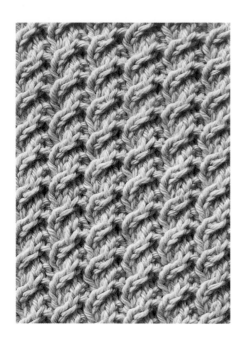

Mock cable I

MULTIPLE OF 8 STITCHES PLUS 1

Easier than it looks, this attractive pattern uses three-stitch twists.

Mock cable II

MULTIPLE OF 5 STITCHES PLUS 2

Simple twist stitches on the right side and purl rows on the wrong side make an easy stitch with plenty of texture.

Twisted rib

MULTIPLE OF 4 STITCHES PLUS 2

(WS) P into front of 2nd st on left needle, p into first st, sl both sts off needle tog.

Twisting together two stitches on every row makes a firm, well-defined rib.

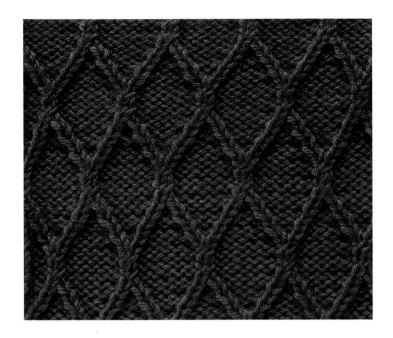

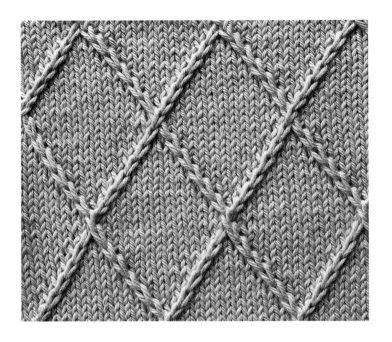

Two-twist lattice

MULTIPLE OF 8 STITCHES PLUS 2

For a three-twist lattice, simply work rows 1 and 2 twice, then rows 3 to 10. Work rows 11 and 12 twice, then rows 13 to 20, making a 24-row repeat.

For a wider lattice, work on a multiple of 10 stitches, allowing two more purl stitches between twists on the first row, then moving the stitches four times to create the diamond shapes.

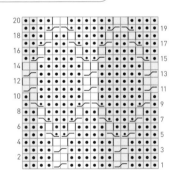

Slip stitch lattice

MULTIPLE OF 14 STITCHES PLUS 2

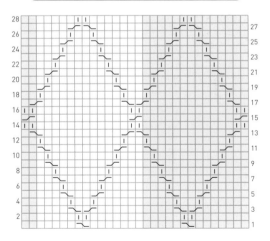

Slipping the traveling stitches on wrong-side rows makes them lie smoothly, and because they are stretched over two rows, they can be seen clearly even though the background is stockinette stitch.

KEY TO CHART SYMBOLS pages 140–141

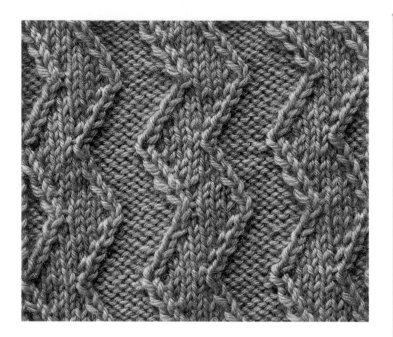

Zigzags

```
MULTIPLE OF 12 STITCHES
```

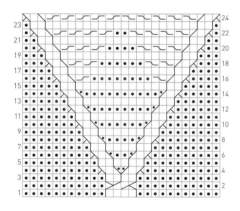

Stockinette stitch zigzags are outlined with twisted stitches for more definition and surface texture.

Inverted pyramids

```
PANEL OF 26 STITCHES
```

The twisted stitches inside the inverted pyramids could be cabled, but twisting them gives a smoother texture.

Slip stitch diagonals

MULTIPLE OF 16 STITCHES PLUS 7

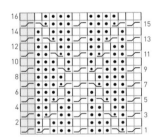

Slipping the traveling stitches on the previous row elongates and gives extra definition to these diagonals and ribs.

Wave and twist

MULTIPLE OF 14 STITCHES PLUS 2

Twist stitches are good for giving the effect of Aran knitting in miniature.

KEY TO CHART SYMBOLS pages 140–141

Twist stitch band

MULTIPLE OF 4 STITCHES PLUS 7

This band appears to sit on the surface of the knitting because of the increases in the first row and the decreases that are made in the last row.

▼ Increase 2 sts by working [k1, yo, k1] in st.

△ Decrease 2 sts by working ssk, then sl rem st back onto left needle and pass 2nd st on needle over.

Skeleton leaf

MOTIF OF 23 STITCHES

Slipped traveling stitches make a skeleton leaf pattern against a subtle knit and purl textured shape.

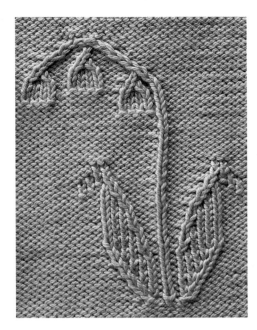

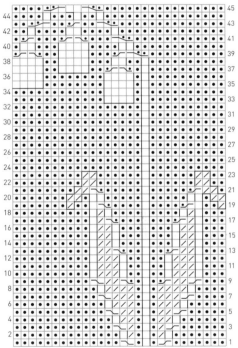

Branching leaves

PANEL OF 27 STITCHES

Bellflower motif

MOTIF OF 28 STITCHES

Since you cannot really knit stitches horizontally, you will need to embroider two chain stitches to complete the curve at the top of the stem when you have finished knitting. The rest of the motif is surprisingly simple.

You will find this 20-row repeat quite easy to follow, even though you do need to watch out for twists on the wrong-side rows.

KEY TO CHART SYMBOLS pages 140–141

LACE

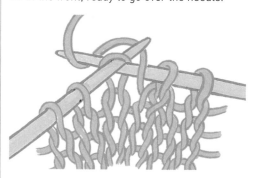

LACE STITCH PATTERNS ARE SIMPLY A COMBINATION OF DECREASES AND OPEN INCREASES. THE NEW STITCHES ARE MADE BY TAKING THE YARN OVER THE NEEDLE, CREATING A LIGHT AND AIRY EFFECT.

The easiest lace patterns have each increase worked next to the corresponding decrease, so the stitch count stays the same on every row. In other patterns, the increases and decreases occur at different places along the row, but you will find these just as easy to work because the total number of stitches on each row does not change. For some beautiful laces, the increases and decreases are made on different rows, making it harder to keep track of the stitch count, but creating exquisite patterns.

The choice of yarn affects the appearance of lace knitting. Firm, smooth yarns make the design more visible; soft or brushed yarns blur the pattern. Traditionally, very fine wool or cotton is worked on relatively large needles. When the work is pinned and blocked, the delicate texture of the lace is revealed.

MAKING A YARN OVER

It is essential to take the yarn over the needle so that the strand lies in the same direction as the other stitches. Working into this strand on the next row makes a hole, but if the strand is twisted, the hole will close up. When the stitch before a yarn over is purl, the yarn will already be at the front, ready to go over the needle.

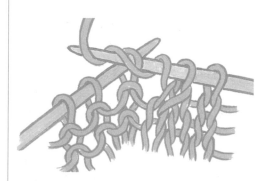

To make a yarn over between two knit stitches, bring the yarn to the front as if to purl, then take it over the needle to knit the next stitch.

To make a yarn over between a knit and a purl stitch, bring the yarn to the front as if to purl, then take it over the needle and bring it to the front again, ready to purl.

LACE TOP AND SCARF
Fine yarns have been used to great effect for these examples of Shetland lace knitting—a style of very fine, elaborate lace knitting originating from the Shetland Islands, Scotland.

SEE ALSO
••••••••••••
• Creating your own designs, pages 50–57
• Lace stitch patterns, pages 102–109

MAKING MULTIPLE YARN OVERS

Some lace patterns have larger holes made by working two or more yarn overs together. The extra yarn overs may be dropped on the following row, so that only one stitch is increased, or they may all be worked so that several stitches are made.

Bring the yarn to the front, then take it over the needle. Repeat this process for each of the remaining yarn overs, then work the next stitch.

SIMPLE ALLOVER FAGGOT LACE

A very open-mesh texture is made over an even number of stitches by working yarn over, knit two stitches together along every row.

CREATING LACE PATTERNS

Designing a lace stitch pattern is easier that it may seem. Start by looking at the charted examples in this book. In order to prevent the knitted fabric from getting progressively wider by the addition of yarn overs, there needs to be an equal number of decreased stitches. Each row does not have to end with the same number of stitches, but the number of stitches at the start of the stitch pattern repeat and at the end should be the same. The distance between a decrease and a yarn over is also an important factor in lace design—placing them next to each other or spaced apart will create different effects. In addition, working increases and decreases only on right-side rows creates a different effect from patterning on every row.

When you are ready to start designing, begin by charting the position of the yarn overs and the areas of more solid knitting, then position the decreases. However, as with all knit design, the only way to understand the fabric you are creating is to knit a swatch.

DECREASES NEXT TO YARN OVERS

The decreases are worked immediately to one side of the yarn overs and add sharp definition to the zigzag.

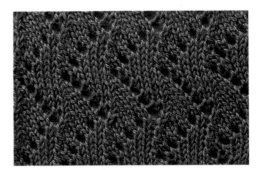

DECREASES AND YARN OVERS SPACED APART

The decreases are worked a few stitches away from the yarn overs and so create gently wandering lines up the fabric.

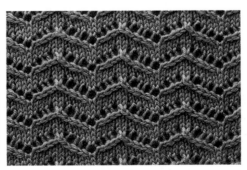

DECREASES AND YARN OVERS ON EVERY ROW

The patterning is on every row, giving a lacier appearance as well as a less sharply angled chevron.

DECREASES AND YARN OVERS ON ALTERNATE ROWS

The steep angle of these chevrons is the result of patterning on alternate rows.

Feather and fan

MULTIPLE OF 14 STITCHES PLUS 1

◢ K4 tog.

◣ Sl 2 knitwise, k2 tog tbl,
    pass sl sts over.

This is an old Shetland lace stitch pattern
with many variations. Common to them all
is the grouping of increases and decreases
separately from each other along the row
to make patterns resembling feathers,
fans, waves, and scallops.

Cabled feather

MULTIPLE OF 19 STITCHES PLUS 2

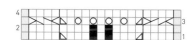

Cables have been added to this feather
and fan pattern. Some of the decreases are
worked two rows away from the increases,
resulting in a different stitch count in two
of the rows.

Old shale

MULTIPLE OF 18 STITCHES PLUS 1

This version of a famous Shetland lace
stitch is particularly simple and rhythmic.

Lace ladder

MULTIPLE OF 4 STITCHES PLUS 2

Very smooth and
controlled, this
ladder is quite
stable in spite of
its open texture.

Bird's eye

MULTIPLE OF 4 STITCHES PLUS 4

Allover double eyelets
make an unusually
textured lace pattern.

Scotch faggot cable

MULTIPLE OF 12 STITCHES PLUS 8

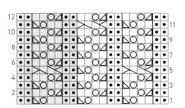

Cabling a faggot rib creates a stitch that
can be used as an allover repeat or in
conjunction with other open stitches.

KEY TO CHART SYMBOLS **pages 140–141**

Leaves and berries

PANEL OF 21 STITCHES PLUS 2

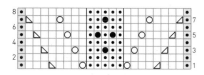

● [K1, p1, k1, p1, k1] all into one st, making 5 sts from one, turn, p5, turn, lift 2nd, 3rd, 4th, and 5th sts over first and off needle, k st tbl.

Bobbles are very compatible with many lace stitches. Here, clusters of bobbles have been added to a leaf stitch.

Tulip

PANEL OF 13 STITCHES

Many pictorial effects can be achieved with lace stitches—this tulip is slightly embossed.

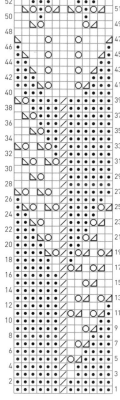

Small heart I

MOTIF OF 11 STITCHES

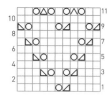

This simple heart could be used as a repeat pattern or scattered among other motifs.

Small heart II

MOTIF OF 13 STITCHES

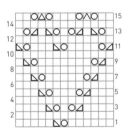

△ K2 tog, return st to left needle, pass next st over it, sl st back onto right needle.

This heart motif could also be used as a leaf motif.

Pierced heart

MOTIF OF 21 STITCHES

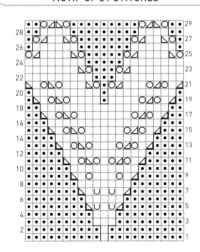

Yarn overs and their corresponding decreases help to shape this heart as well as decorate it.

Picot heart

MOTIF OF 24 STITCHES

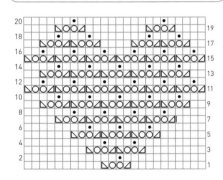

The double eyelets that make this heart motif have a heart shape themselves, made by working p1, k1 into the double yarn over, instead of the usual k1, p1.

KEY TO CHART SYMBOLS pages 140–141

Diamond spiral

PANEL OF 15 STITCHES

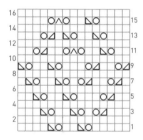

This simple but sophisticated panel would work well alongside cables.

Candlelight

MULTIPLE OF 10 STITCHES PLUS 11

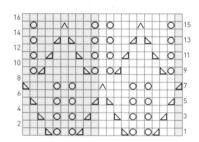

Lace knitting lends itself to flame- and leaf-like patterns. In each of these motifs, the decreases move away from the increases, pulling the stitches into outlines.

Falling leaves

MULTIPLE OF 10 STITCHES PLUS 11

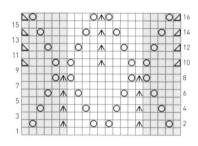

This is similar to the candlelight pattern (left) in construction, but the decreases pull the stitches in to form the central vein of each leaf.

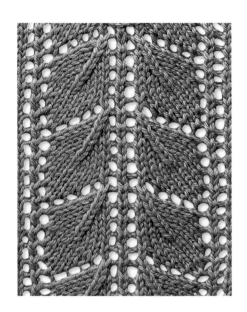

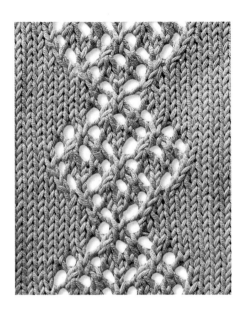

Feather lace

MULTIPLE OF 8 STITCHES PLUS 11

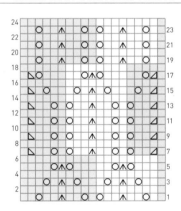

Here, increases outline long, feather-like shapes.

Paired leaves

PANEL OF 29 STITCHES

The increases and decreases form drooping leaves with veins and make the lower edge strongly shaped.

Clustered leaves

PANEL OF 13 STITCHES

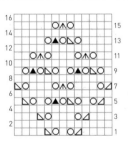

▲ K3 tog.

Repeating all 16 rows of this chart makes an attractive panel. A single repeat makes a large motif, or one of the leaves can easily be adapted to make a tiny motif.

Gothic lace

MULTIPLE OF 8 STITCHES PLUS 1

This is a progression of the feather lace pattern on page 107. One repeat of the chart makes a border, while repeating rows 1 to 16 produces an allover pattern.

Leaf cascade

MULTIPLE OF 16 STITCHES PLUS 17

Despite the background being very open, this is not a difficult stitch to knit, but note the use of two different double decreases.

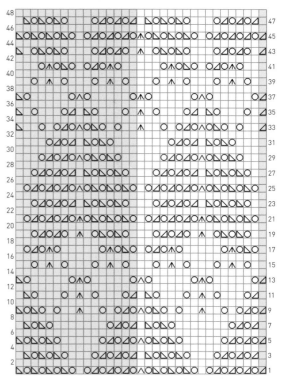

Fern edging

CAST ON 10 STITCHES

This leafy edging in garter stitch has large eyelets made with multiple yarn overs.

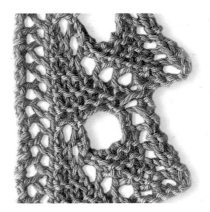

--- Bind off.

✽ St remaining after binding off.

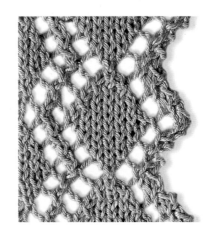

Mesh lace edging

CAST ON 14 STITCHES

This pattern is based on garter stitch, so either side can be used as the right side. This picture shows the smooth side.

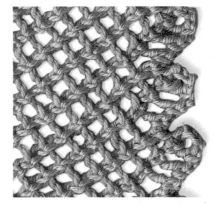

--- Bind off.

✽ St remaining after binding off.

Diamond edging

CAST ON 10 STITCHES

This is a classic edging that has many uses. Careful pressing is required to open out the lace. After working rows 1 to 14, repeat only rows 3 to 14.

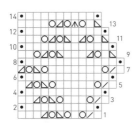

BOBBLES AND LEAVES

INCREASES AND DECREASES CAN BE USED TO EMBELLISH A KNITTED SURFACE WITH THREE-DIMENSIONAL STITCHES, CREATING A VARIETY OF INTERESTING EFFECTS.

A group of increased stitches, decreased abruptly, makes a knot or a bobble that can be used to add emphasis to a familiar cable or lace pattern. Bobbles, knots, and leaves are often worked on a reverse stockinette background to emphasize the contrast.

Knots are worked into one stitch and completed without turning the work. Bobbles are also worked into one stitch but have extra rows added by turning and working the bobble stitches only. Different size bobbles can be scattered or clustered according to the design.

Both knots and bobbles are worked into a single stitch and are completed before the next stitch on the left needle is worked. Leaf designs are often constructed in the same way as bobble stitch combinations, but the stitches are worked over several rows.

There is also a family of allover textured popcorn and blackberry stitches that are made from repeated groups of increases and decreases that alternate on following rows.

SEE ALSO

- Basic cast-ons, pages 16–17
- Decreases and increases, pages 28–34
- Texture and color, page 56
- Bobble and leaf stitch patterns, pages 112–119

MAKING A THREE-STITCH KNOT
Knots are always made on right-side rows.

1 Cast on three stitches by working as for a cable cast-on, but work into the front of the previous stitch rather than in the space between stitches.

2 Knit the three cast-on stitches, then knit the original stitch again, making four new stitches on the right needle.

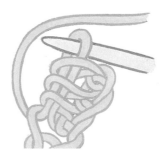

3 To complete the knot, lift three stitches, one at a time, over the last stitch on the right needle.

PARTY DRESS
Bobbles and leaves are a feature of this pretty outfit.

MAKING A FIVE-STITCH BOBBLE

Bobbles are always started on a right-side row.

1 Into a stitch, work [k1, yarn over needle] twice, then k1 again, making five stitches on the right needle.

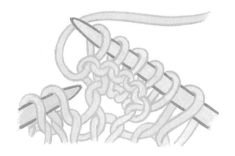

2 Then turn and purl the five stitches. Turn and knit five stitches.

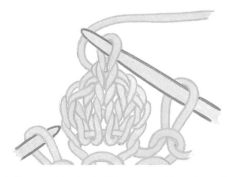

3 To complete the bobble, turn, p2 together, p1, p2 together, turn, slip 2 knitwise, k1, pass the slipped stitches over. As a variation, complete the bobble by lifting the stitches over in the same way as the three-stitch knot opposite.

KNOTS AND BOBBLES

The top line shows three-stitch knots; the three sizes of bobbles below are worked using five and seven stitches over different numbers of rows.

MAKING THE PERFECT BOBBLE

Always read the pattern instructions carefully. There are more bobbles than most designers can name or chart illustrators create unique symbols for. A familiar symbol may not represent the same process as the last time you saw it.

Knit the edge stitches firmly and adjust them with the needle tip as necessary.

In general, it is better not to work a bobble too tightly. This makes it easier to work and results in a fluffy, pleasing bobble. If the first stitch after a bobble is baggy, knit into the back of it—the twisted stitch will be hidden by the bobble.

If making a large bobble, you may find it easier to use a third needle to work the bobble—perhaps one slightly larger. Look for one with a sharp tip.

MAKING A SEVEN-STITCH LEAF

Larger groups of decorative increases and decreases worked over several rows make a blister—a flat, raised shape—or a leaf that can be used as part of a motif or be integrated into a stitch pattern. The three leaves below are the same size but each made slightly differently. In all of them, pairs of increases are followed by pairs of decreases, worked at the sides or in the center.

Creating a leaf with a vein effect

This leaf has yarn overs each side of the center stitch. The base of the leaf conforms easily to the fabric around it.

Creating a firmer leaf shape

Lifted-strand increases each side of the center stitch are used to shape the base of the leaf. This type of leaf shape is raised from the fabric around it.

Creating a softer, smooth leaf shape

Seven stitches are worked into a double yarn over at the start of this leaf. This type of leaf shape is raised from the fabric around it and is maleable.

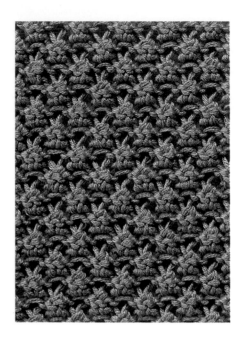

Blackberry stitch

MULTIPLE OF 4 STITCHES

V̄ [K1, p1, k1] all into one st, making 3 sts from one.

△ P3 tog.

This allover nubbly pattern is also known as trinity stitch, because three stitches are made from one and one from three on alternate rows.

Knotted rib

MULTIPLE OF 6 STITCHES PLUS 2

◉ K into front, back, and front of st, making 3 sts from one, lift 2nd and first sts over 3rd and off needle.

Here, the very smallest possible knot adds texture to the smooth surface of a rib stitch worked through the back of the loops.

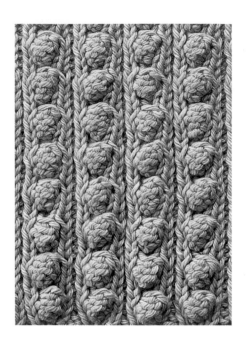

Bobble rib

MULTIPLE OF 5 STITCHES PLUS 2

◎ [K1, yo, k1, yo, k1] all into one st, making 5 sts from one, turn, k5, turn, p5, lift 4th, 3rd, 2nd, and first sts over 5th and off needle.

Crunchy bobbles are worked so closely together in this pattern that they make the rib spread out instead of pulling in.

Bobble blocks

MULTIPLE OF 6 STITCHES PLUS 1

5 [K1, yo, k1, yo, k1] all into one st, making 5 sts from one, turn, k5, turn, skpo, k3 tog, lift first st over 2nd and off needle.

Purl stitch bobbles are placed in regular rows on stockinette stitch blocks, and outlined in alternating knit and purl stitches.

Bobble and wave

MULTIPLE OF 8 STITCHES

⊙ [K1, yo, k1, yo, k1] all into one st, making 5 sts from one, turn, k5, turn, p5, lift 4th, 3rd, 2nd, and first sts over 5th and off needle.

The wave rib is not cabled; it is made with increases and decreases. The bobbles add an accent at the curve of each wave.

Triple nosegay

MULTIPLE OF 17 STITCHES PLUS 1

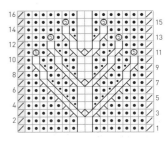

⊙ [K1, yo, k1, yo, k1] all into one st, making 5 sts from one, turn, k5, turn, p5, lift 4th, 3rd, 2nd, and first sts over 5th and off needle.

The traditional nosegay pattern has just two branches with four bobbles. Work through the chart a few times, and you may see how to make a nosegay pattern with even more branches.

KEY TO CHART SYMBOLS pages 140–141

Wave and knots cable

MULTIPLE OF 8 STITCHES

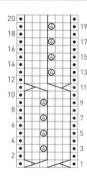

⑤ K into front and back of st twice, making 4 sts from one, lift 3rd, 2nd, and first sts over 4th and off needle.

Knots are faster to work than bobbles because you do not have to turn the work. You could substitute the large knot shown here with any of the smaller bobbles from other designs.

Three-bobble cable

MULTIPLE OF 10 STITCHES PLUS 1

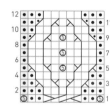

⑤ [K1, yo, k1, yo, k1] all into one st, making 5 sts from one, turn, k5, turn, p5, lift 4th, 3rd, 2nd, and first sts over 5th and off needle.

Cabled ovals enclose three crunchy, purl stitch bobbles. The large cable cross uses five stitches (an odd number) to give a center stitch on which to position the bobbles.

Strawberry bobble

MULTIPLE OF 12 STITCHES PLUS 1

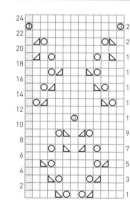

③ [K1, yo, k1] all into one st, making 3 sts from one, turn, k3, turn, p3, lift 2nd and first sts over 3rd and off needle.

Bobbles can be used as an accent on lace stitches as well as cables. The berry motifs are arranged as a half-drop pattern here, but it would be easy to make a panel by repeating just the first 12 rows.

Large leaf and twists

◯ MULTIPLE OF 26 STITCHES PLUS 1 ◯

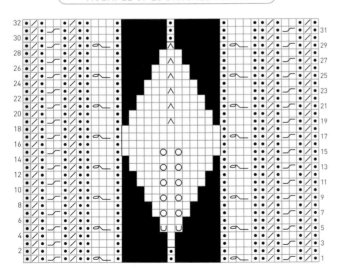

Sl 1 purlwise, k1,
yo, k1, lift sl st over
the k1, yo, k1 and
off needle.

The little twists at each side of the leaf are very simple, but as
the leaf expands and contracts it curves the twists, making
the pattern look more complicated than it really is.

Bobble and braid cable

◯ PANEL OF 29 STITCHES ◯

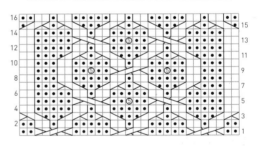

◎ [K1, yo, k1, yo, k1] all into one st, making
5 sts from one, turn, k5, turn, p5, lift 4th, 3rd,
2nd, and first sts over 5th and off needle.

This cable panel uses a five-stitch cross, so there
is a center stitch on which to place the bobble.

KEY TO CHART SYMBOLS pages 140–141

Heart leaf

MOTIF OF 11 STITCHES

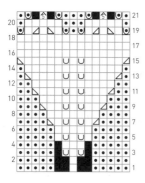

[Sl 1 knitwise] twice, [sl 1 purlwise, lift 1 st over and off right needle, sl st back onto left needle, lift 1 st over and off left needle] twice, p st that remains.

The surface of this motif is only slightly raised because most of the increases have compensating decreases.

Bell pattern

MULTIPLE OF 4 STITCHES PLUS 4

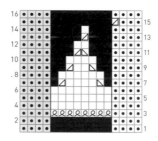

Cast on 1 st using backward loop cast-on method, twisting the loop before placing it on the needle.

To work a frilled edging from this chart, cast on a multiple of 12 stitches plus 4, then starting with the third row, k8 where the cast-on stitches are indicated. Follow the chart to make the bell shapes and you will end with a stitch count that is a multiple of four.

Puff stitch

MULTIPLE OF 10 STITCHES PLUS 2

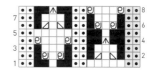

Use left needle to lift strand between sts from the front, then knit into front of it to increase 1 st and make a small hole beneath.

Regular increases and decreases give a slightly raised surface to this pattern but it is easy to work because, despite making and losing stitches on each right-side row, the stitch count remains constant.

Flower sprigs

MULTIPLE OF 14 STITCHES PLUS 1

These pretty little motifs have slender leaves because the open increases are taken into the reverse stockinette stitch background.

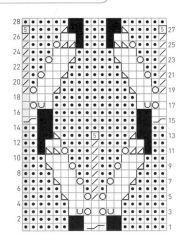

⑤   [K1, yo, k1, yo, k1] all into one st, making 5 sts from one, turn, p5, turn, k5, lift 4th, 3rd, 2nd, and first sts over 5th and off needle.

Cable with leaf and bobbles

PANEL OF 25 STITCHES

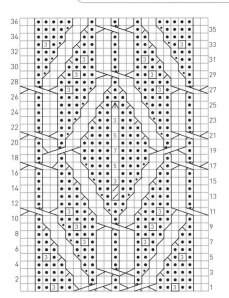

③   K into front, back, and front of st, making 3 sts from one, turn, p3, turn, k3, lift 2nd and first sts over 3rd and off needle.

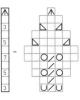

Work supplementary leaf chart each time the 1-stitch, 11-row symbol is indicated.

The leaf is given a separate chart to make it easier to follow the cable pattern.

KEY TO CHART SYMBOLS **pages 140–141**

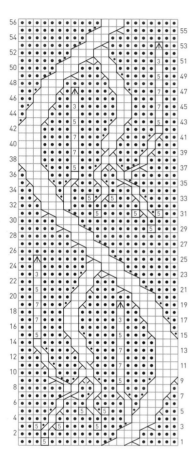

Celtic vine

PANEL OF 21 STITCHES

Inspired by tree-of-life carvings on early stone crosses, this design has a separate small chart for the leaf to make it easier to follow the chart when working the curved, cabled stem.

Work supplementary leaf chart each time the 1-stitch, 11-row symbol is indicated.

5 [K1, yo, k1, yo, k1] all into one st, making 5 sts from one, turn, p5, turn, k5, turn, p2 tog, p1, p2 tog, turn, sl 2 sts as if to work k2 tog, k1, pass sl sts over.

Afterthought flower

PANEL OF 9 STITCHES AND 12 ROWS

This very adaptable motif is not quite an afterthought because you do need to plan enough seed stitch background and place the bobbles. A minimum of 3in (7cm) in seed stitch is needed all around the bobble area to place the petals. You could vary the size and number of petals to suit the scale of your yarn.

Work each marked stitch as k on RS and p on WS for the seed stitch background. When you have finished knitting the background, lift the stitch indicated and work (k1, yo, k1) into it for the first row of the supplementary petal chart. Continue working the petal, detached from the background, then fasten off and sew in place.

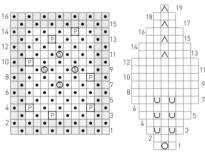

P   Lift stitch and work supplementary petal chart.

S   [K1, yo, k1, yo, k1] all into one st, making 5 sts from one, turn, p5, turn, k5, lift 4th, 3rd, 2nd, and first sts over 5th and off needle.

KEY TO CHART SYMBOLS pages 140–141

STRANDED COLOR KNITTING

ALL AROUND THE WORLD, PEOPLE HAVE DEVELOPED TRADITIONS OF COLOR KNITTING. AMONG THE BEST KNOWN ARE PATTERNS FROM FAIR ISLE, SCANDINAVIA, EASTERN EUROPE, AND SOUTH AMERICA.

SEE ALSO
....
• Color in design, pages 54–55
• Stranded color stitch patterns, pages 122–129

Most stranded color knitting is worked in stockinette with just two colors in a row. One or both of these colors may be changed on subsequent rows. Some patterns use three or even four colors in a row, but this can make the fabric very thick.

Stranded color knitting is usually worked from a chart. Reading the chart as directed, count the squares in the first color, and work that number of stitches. Then count and work the stitches in the second color. Continue counting and changing the colors along the row. Once you have established the first row, you can simply glance at the chart to see how the motifs change.

In many traditions, stranded color knitting is worked in the round, making it easy to see the pattern. If you are color knitting in the round, read each row of the chart from right to left. As you will discover, most traditional Fair Isle patterns change color after no more than seven stitches in a row, with the yarn not in use stranded loosely on the wrong side of the work. Stranding across more stitches would make an over-long strand, so it is best if the yarn not in use is woven in at regular intervals to keep the wrong side tidy.

YARNS
Use different yarns to change the character of your design. Using a variegated yarn can produce the visual richness of frequent color changes, but without all the yarn ends you would get from using several single-color balls of yarn.

HOLDING THE YARNS
The simplest way to change colors is to drop one yarn and pick up the other. However, for faster knitting, experiment with the following techniques.

HOLDING ONE YARN IN EACH HAND
Hold and work with one yarn in the right hand in your preferred way (see pages 14–15), and the other yarn tensioned through the fingers of your left hand. To knit with the left-hand yarn, insert the right needle, dip it under the yarn, and pull it through with a hook-like action. When purling, take care not to twist stitches.

HOLDING BOTH YARNS IN ONE HAND
Hold both the yarns in the right hand, with the main color over the first finger and the contrast color tensioned over the middle finger. Knit in the usual way with the main color, then turn the hand slightly to flick the yarn from the middle finger around the needle for the contrast stitches. On purl rows, you may find it easier to manipulate the main color between thumb and first finger, and hold the contrast over the first finger.

WORKING WITH MORE THAN ONE YARN

Although this style of knitting involves working with more than one yarn, only one yarn is actually knitted at any one time—the other is looped or carried across the wrong side of the work until it is next required. Depending on the stitch pattern, the yarn not in use can be carried along the row by stranding or weaving the yarn on the wrong side of the work.

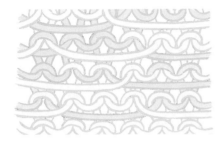

STRANDING

If the yarn is not going to be in use for only a few stitches, then stranding is the best option. The strands carried across should be tensioned loosely and evenly so that the knitting lies flat. Decide which color will lie on top and always strand the yarns in the same order.

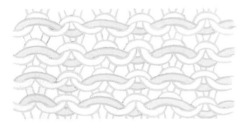

WEAVING

If the yarn is not going to be in use for more than five to seven stitches, then weaving is the best option. The yarn not in use is woven over and under, making a very firm fabric. Take care that the contrast color does not show through to the right side.

TWISTING THE YARNS

An alternative to stranding or weaving is to twist the yarns around each other; see how to link color areas on page 131.

CHILD'S JACKET AND BERET

Stranded color knitting can be worked in rows or in rounds.

SHORT REPEAT PATTERNS

These little geometric patterns are called peerie patterns.

FAIR ISLE PATTERNS

The northern coast of Scotland has a strong tradition of color knitting referred to as Fair Isle. The rich use of color often makes stitch patterns appear very intricate, but they usually have short repeats and use only two colors in each row. One yarn is often described as the background yarn and the other as the motif yarn, and each of these may be changed every row or few rows.

USE OF COLOR

This star motif is instantly recognizable as a Fair Isle pattern by the shaded effect. The color changes may take the form of a gradual progression, with the occasional surprise contrast color, or a more dramatic color sequence may be worked.

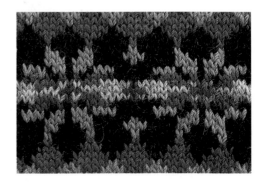

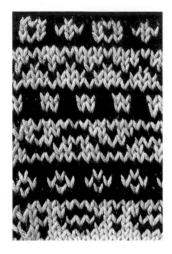

MULTIPLE OF 20 STS PLUS 1

MULTIPLE OF 8 STS PLUS 1

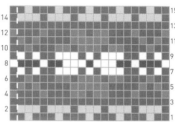

MULTIPLE OF 20 STS PLUS 1

MULTIPLE OF 4 STS PLUS 1

MULTIPLE OF 4 STS PLUS 1

MULTIPLE OF 8 STS PLUS 1

Peerie patterns

Little two- and three-row patterns like these are often used as a contrast between more complex bands of motifs. However, they can also be used as allover stitch patterns. Have fun varying the colors on a striped or plain background for an easy-to-knit version of classic Fair Isle.

Flower borders

Some of these small borders are built up out of peerie patterns, while others stand alone. Here, the background is all one shade, but for a more authentic color scheme, change the background for each band of pattern.

MULTIPLE OF 12 STS PLUS 1

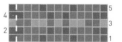

MULTIPLE OF 4 STS PLUS 1

MULTIPLE OF 8 STS PLUS 1

MULTIPLE OF 8 STS PLUS 1

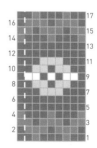

Starflower with diamond flower border

(MULTIPLE OF 20 STITCHES PLUS 1)

Instead of gently shading the colors of either the background or motif yarns, here the color changes in the motif and background are made on the same row. This adds to the jazzy feel of this bright interpretation of a traditional star with peerie patterns.

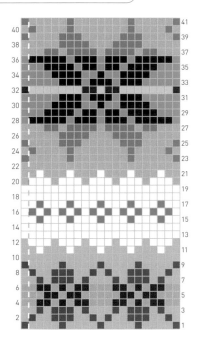

Armada crosses

(MULTIPLE OF 24 STITCHES PLUS 1)

The first band of pattern shows a simple version of the cross; the second is more complex. Both of these are variations on X and O patterns. For an allover pattern, continue traveling the double line of yellow stitches over the navy background on rows 12, 13, and 14, then on rows 34, 35, and 36 to join up the X motifs.

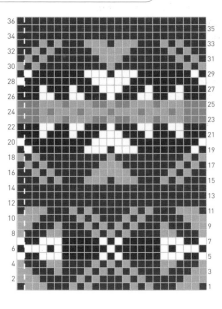

KEY TO CHART SYMBOLS   pages 140–141

Scandinavian stripes

MULTIPLE OF 4 STITCHES PLUS 1

Worked in monochrome—
black and white, or brown
and natural—these
versatile patterns are
typically Scandinavian,
but if you shade the
background, they will
look like Fair Isle. Similar
patterns in solid, bright
colors can be found on
Turkish socks.

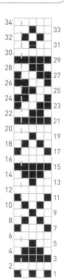

Snowflake border and flea pattern

MULTIPLE OF 24 STITCHES PLUS 1

The flea pattern at the top of this sample
is a simple seeding pattern that can be
varied with many different spacings,
depending on the repeat of the pattern it is
worked with. If you want to work the pretty
Norwegian snowflake as an allover pattern,
simply repeat rows 9 to 32.

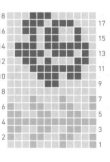

Rosebuds and ivy

MULTIPLE OF 10 STITCHES PLUS 1

These very pretty patterns are inspired by Swedish mittens. Work rows 17 to 26 for just one row of rosebuds, or repeat rows 17 to 38 for an allover pattern.

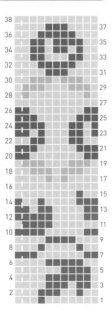

Harebells and vine

MULTIPLE OF 12 STITCHES PLUS 1

The vine borders are shown running in opposite directions. If you want to knit the next band of harebells with the flowers facing right, read rows 9 to 31 in the opposite direction.

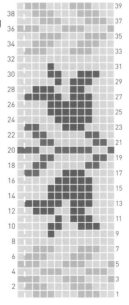

Roses and vine

MULTIPLE OF 12 STITCHES

To space the rose motif as in the swatch, begin each subsequent repeat of the 9th row five stitches in from the right of the chart. Work the 10-row rose motif twelve times before the pattern repeats exactly on row 121.

KEY TO CHART SYMBOLS pages 140–141

Latvian morning stars

MULTIPLE OF 16 STITCHES PLUS 1

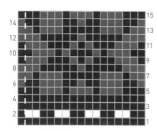

Use this striking star as a border or arrange it as a half-drop allover pattern, as shown above.

Large reindeer

MULTIPLE OF 30 STITCHES PLUS 1

Although most of this pattern has been designed for stranded knitting, you may find it easier to use separate balls of yarn for some sections of the design.

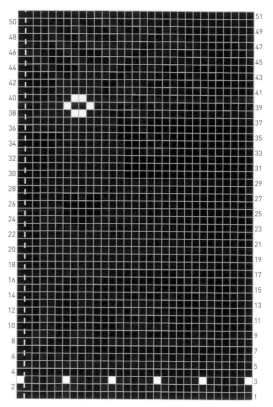

Latvian stars

MULTIPLE OF 18 STITCHES PLUS 1

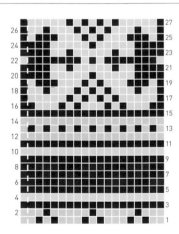

A series of stacked, geometric border patterns contrasting with an allover design are typical of the patterns found on Latvian mittens. This design is quite easy to knit, because only row 22 has more than two colors.

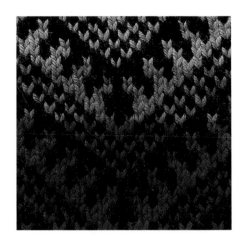

Turkish sock pattern

MULTIPLE OF 12 STITCHES PLUS 1

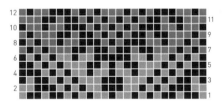

Each side of the center stitch is a mirror image of the other, and the multiple of 12 stitches is counted each side of the center stitch. Here, the background color is changed every six rows, but you could use just one color or change the background as often as you wish.

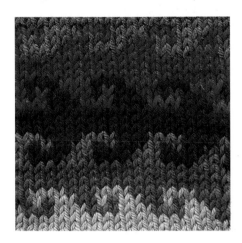

Turkish arrowhead

MULTIPLE OF 6 STITCHES PLUS 1

This pattern is easy to knit, but capable of subtle variation. Try reversing the direction of the motif on a striped background.

KEY TO CHART SYMBOLS pages 140–141

Star with shaded waves

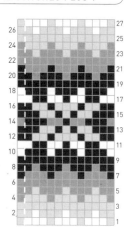

MULTIPLE OF 12 STITCHES PLUS 1

This little star shows how the tone of the colors you use can emphasize the motif. When choosing colors to work this motif, make sure that you substitute your darkest shade for the brown, moving through to the lightest shade for the warm white.

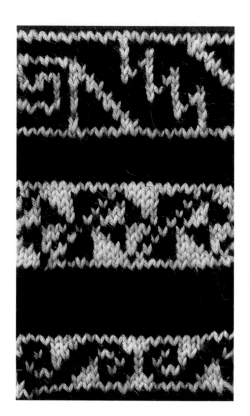

Geometric patterns

These geometric designs originate from South America. The large lightning pattern is based on an embroidery design. If you would like to work a brighter version of this pattern, try working each lightning and key motif in a different color. The smaller paddle and scroll motifs are similar to popular designs used in weaving.

MULTIPLE OF 29 STITCHES PLUS 1

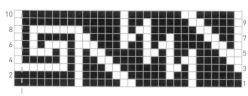

MULTIPLE OF 10 STS PLUS 1

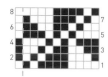

MULTIPLE OF 14 STS PLUS 1

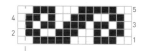

Sawtooth border

MULTIPLE OF 5 STITCHES PLUS 1

Motifs similar to this South American geometric repeat can be found on pottery and basketwork, as well as knitting. They are often used in the same way as peerie patterns in a Fair Isle.

South American waves

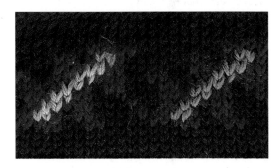

MULTIPLE OF 8 STITCHES PLUS 1

Use this simple geometric pattern to move from one area of solid color to another.

Peruvian leaf border

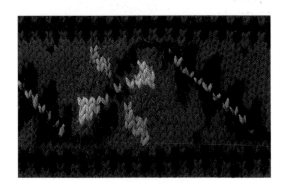

MULTIPLE OF 13 STITCHES PLUS 2

Strand the yarns for the purple background and pink leaf motifs, but use separate short lengths of contrasting color for each diagonal leaf vein. Change the contrasting color as often as you like.

Peruvian flower border

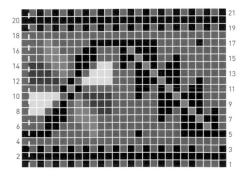

MULTIPLE OF 26 STITCHES PLUS 1

You will need to strand three colors when working this design: pink, navy, and green. Just loop the green over a strand to carry it across the large gaps. The purple and yellow petals are best knitted with separate lengths of yarn. This design is very graphic and would also work well in two colors.

KEY TO CHART SYMBOLS pages 140–141

INTARSIA COLOR KNITTING

LARGE GEOMETRIC PATTERNS, INDIVIDUAL MOTIFS, AND PICTURE KNITS ARE THE KIND OF COLOR DESIGNS THAT ARE BEST KNITTED USING THE INTARSIA TECHNIQUE.

Intarsia is simply working areas of color with separate balls of yarn that are linked together at each color change. This eliminates stranding or weaving in on the wrong side, and gives a single-thickness fabric. The technique is used for flat knitting only—intarsia cannot be worked in the round.

Designs in intarsia are worked from charts where the number of stitches in each color can be seen clearly and easily. Stockinette is the most frequently used stitch, but the technique works just as well with textured stitches such as bobbles, cables, and twists.

Some designs—such as tiny blocks of color scattered on a plain background—are best worked in a combination of intarsia and stranding. Use separate lengths of yarn for small motifs, and strand the background color, twisting the yarns at each color change.

ORGANIZING THE YARNS

First, sort out the yarns by counting the number of areas in each color, then wind off suitable lengths of yarn according to the size of the areas. Use complete balls of yarn for each large area. Wind the yarn onto bobbins for smaller areas or, if there are just a few contrast stitches, use a short length of yarn. If the design is very complex with lots of colors, avoid tangles by using lengths of yarn that can be pulled free easily because they are not attached to a ball or bobbin.

SEE ALSO

- Embroidery, page 49
- Color in design, pages 54–55
- Stranded color knitting, pages 120–121
- Intarsia stitch patterns, pages 132–139

DIAGONAL COLOR CHANGES

It is easy to keep the knitting neat when working diagonals, because the colors move along one stitch each time and therefore linking the yarns at the changeover comes naturally. For very small areas of only a few stitches, it is sometimes easier to use duplicate stitch embroidery.

BOBBINS

Use bobbins to wind off small quantities of yarn. You can buy bobbins or make your own. Alternatively, wind off small amounts of yarn into balls.

YARN QUANTITIES

To calculate how much yarn you should wind onto a bobbin, use the chart to count the number of stitches to be worked with that length of yarn. Wrap some yarn around one of the working needles ten times; this will be enough to work ten stitches. Measure it and use this figure to calculate how much yarn you will need to complete each section of the motif. Always allow about 6in (15cm) for the yarn ends and a bit extra—just in case.

HOW TO LINK COLOR AREAS

Every time you change colors, you must link the areas together or there will be holes in your knitting. All you need to do is twist the yarns on the wrong side.

VERTICAL COLOR CHANGES

When the colors change at the same place on several rows, be particularly careful to twist the yarns neatly and evenly to avoid holes and loose stitches. Go back at the end of the row and, using the the tip of a needle, ease any extra yarn from loose stitches toward the stitches just worked. Weave in ends along the line of color changes and duplicate stitch any tight stitches.

Tip

Reusable peel-off stickers are ideal for keeping your place in a chart. Position them above the row you are working, so that you can see how it relates to the pattern already knitted.

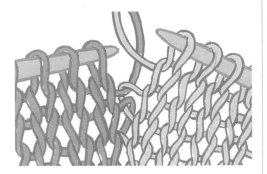

ON A KNIT ROW

Knit with the first color (here, it is pink) to the changeover, then drop the yarn. Pick up the second color (purple) and take it around the first yarn before knitting the next stitch.

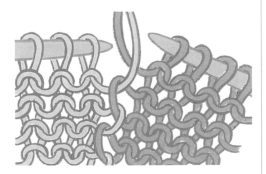

ON A PURL ROW

Purl with the second yarn to the changeover. Make sure that you take the first yarn around the second yarn before knitting the next stitch.

PANSY SWEATER

You can use the intarsia technique to create scattered motifs on a single-color background.

Broken stripes I

MOTIF OF 29 STITCHES

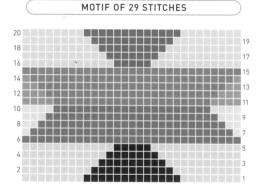

One of the simplest exercises in intarsia is to use a few diagonal color changes to make motifs within stripes. Try light-on-dark or dark-on-light tonal variations. This motif uses darker tones on a background of lighter stripes.

Broken stripes II

MOTIF OF 29 STITCHES

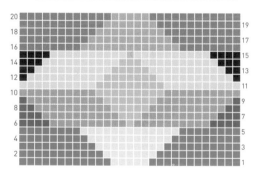

This motif uses lighter tones on a background of darker stripes.

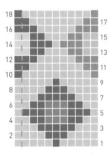

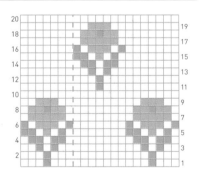

Diamonds

MULTIPLE OF 10 STITCHES PLUS 1

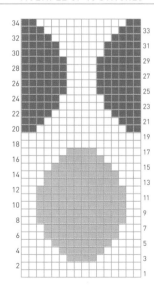

Simple geometric shapes are made more interesting by varying the colors. Instead of being carried along the row horizontally, the colors of the diamonds move diagonally up the design. The color of the square in the center of each diamond changes, and the background is a shaded, brushed mohair yarn.

Spots

MULTIPLE OF 16 STITCHES

Note how the chart image must be elongated to compensate for the proportions of the stockinette stitch.

Sprigs

MULTIPLE OF 14 STITCHES PLUS 7

Even tiny patterns are better worked by the intarsia technique, so that there is no stranding and therefore no double thickness of fabric behind the main background color.

KEY TO CHART SYMBOLS pages 140–141

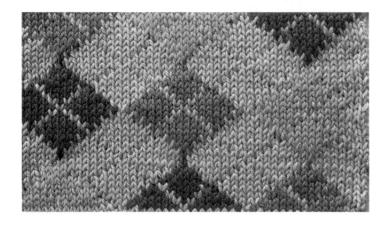

Argyll checks I

MULTIPLE OF 16 STITCHES PLUS 1

Checks and plaids, such as this pattern, are a classic way to use blocks of color. To keep the number of individual lengths of yarn to a minimum, the overchecks can be worked in duplicate stitch embroidery.

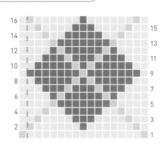

Argyll checks II

MULTIPLE OF 16 STITCHES PLUS 1

The width of the diamonds in this design and the design to the left are the same—they are both 15 stitches wide—but here the width of the diamonds is increased and then reduced by two stitches on every second row worked. In the design on the left, the width of the diamonds is increased and then reduced by two stitches on each row worked.

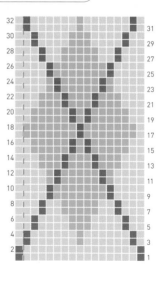

Bugs

These stylized insects are made more lively with a central stripe of a deeper color. Use one or all of them as a repeat pattern or as individual motifs.

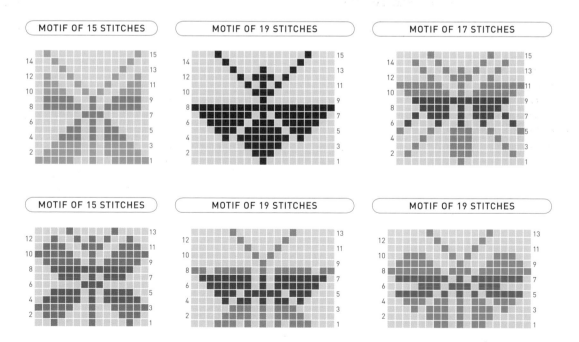

MOTIF OF 15 STITCHES

MOTIF OF 19 STITCHES

MOTIF OF 17 STITCHES

MOTIF OF 15 STITCHES

MOTIF OF 19 STITCHES

MOTIF OF 19 STITCHES

KEY TO CHART SYMBOLS pages 140–141

Scandinavian heart

Danish cross stitch was the inspiration for this crowned heart motif.

MOTIF OF 25 STITCHES

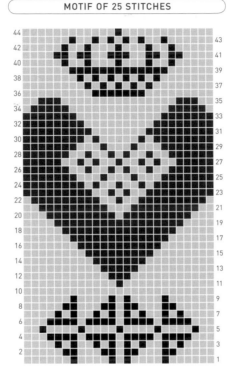

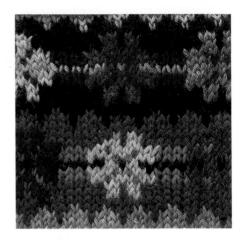

Daisy border

MULTIPLE OF 12 STITCHES PLUS 1

This bright border design has a clear affinity with Fair Isle knitting, but instead of being the same color along the row, the daisies are each in a different color.

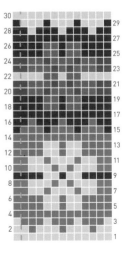

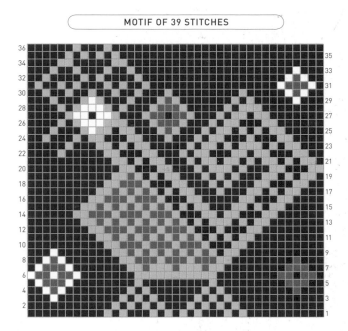

MOTIF OF 39 STITCHES

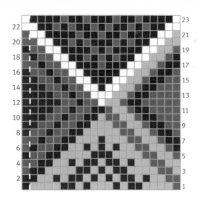

MULTIPLE OF 20 STITCHES PLUS 1

South American bird

Based on a piece of Guatemalan weaving, this
mixture of intarsia and stranded color knitting has
a go-as-you-please border. The geometric repeat
pattern avoids being too mechanical by having
random color changes.

KEY TO CHART SYMBOLS pages 140–141

Chestnut leaves

Organic shapes inspired by
nature can be particularly
successful, because any slight
variance from the image that
inspired you can be classed as
one of nature's imperfections.

MOTIF OF 35 STITCHES

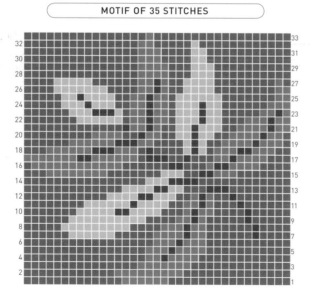

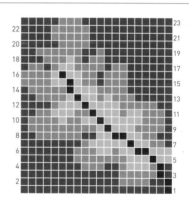

Oak leaf

MOTIF OF 20 STITCHES

Almost any pictorial image can be knitted.
The chart looks taller than the motif
because of the gauge.

Floral vine

> MULTIPLE OF 57 STITCHES

The flower head in this elaborate border design can be varied in color with each pattern repeat.

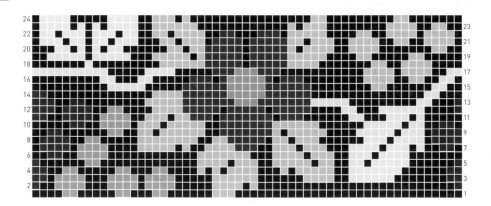

KEY TO CHART SYMBOLS **pages 140–141**

KEY TO PATTERNS

All of the essential information that you will need for using the stitch patterns in this book is gathered here for easy reference.

READING THE CHARTS

Each square of a chart represents one stitch, and each row represents one row of stitches.

The numbers up the sides of a chart are row numbers, and you need to progress from the bottom to the top of the chart.

All rows that are numbered on the right-hand side of a chart are read from that side and represent right-side rows. All rows that are numbered on the left-hand side of a chart are read from that side and represent wrong-side rows.

Black squares on charts are used where stitches do not exist (for example, where a stitch is lost by decreasing and is not compensated for with an increase).

Shaded areas show edge stitches or extra stitches used to balance patterns. Unshaded areas show a panel or the multiple of stitches to repeat. The number of stitches in a panel or multiple is specified for each chart, plus the extra stitches (for example, a multiple of 8 sts plus 2 means multiply 8 by the number of repeats required and then add the 2 end stitches to balance the pattern).

Sometimes stitches are outlined to make reading a chart easier—this does not affect how the stitches are worked.

KEY TO CHART SYMBOLS
The following symbol explanations only apply if another meaning has not been indicated with the stitch pattern.

☐	k on RS rows, p on WS rows
▪	p on RS rows, k on WS rows
◿	k1 tbl on RS rows, p1 tbl on WS rows
■	no stitch
▭	sl 1 wyif on RS rows, sl 1 wyib on WS rows
▭▭	sl 2 wyif on RS rows, sl 2 wyib on WS rows
▭▭▭▭	sl 5 wyib on WS rows
▯	sl 1 wyib on RS rows, sl 1 wyif on WS rows
☑	k in front and back of stitch
�Ս	lift strand between stitches and k into back of it
⍖	lift strand between stitches and p into back of it
◯	yarn forward and over needle to make a stitch
◿	k2 tog
◿	p2 tog
◺	sl 1 knitwise, k1, pass sl st over
◬	sl 1 knitwise, k2 tog, pass sl st over
⋏	sl 2 sts as if to work k2 tog, k1, pass sl sts over
⧄⧅	sl 1 st onto cable needle and hold at back, k1, then k1 from cable needle
⧅⧄	sl 1 st onto cable needle and hold at front, k1, then k1 from cable needle
⧄⧅	on either RS or WS rows, sl 1 st onto cable needle and hold at back, p1, then k1 from cable
⧅⧄	on either RS or WS rows, sl 1 st onto cable needle and hold at front, p1, then k1 from cable needle

sl 2 sts onto cable needle and hold at back, k1, then p2 from cable needle

sl 1 st onto cable needle and hold at front, p2, then k1 from cable needle

sl 1 st onto cable needle and hold at back, k2, then p1 from cable needle

sl 1 st onto cable needle and hold at front, p1, then k2 from cable needle

sl 2 sts onto cable needle and hold at back, k2, then k2 from cable needle

sl 2 sts onto cable needle and hold at front, k2, then k2 from cable needle

sl 2 sts onto cable needle and hold at back, k2, then p2 from cable needle

sl 2 sts onto cable needle and hold at front, p2, then k2 from cable needle

sl 1 st onto cable needle and hold at back, k3, then p1 from cable needle

sl 3 sts onto cable needle and hold at front, p1, then k3 from cable needle

sl 3 sts onto cable needle and hold at back, k2, sl 1 st from cable needle onto left needle and p this st, k2 from cable needle

sl 3 sts onto cable needle and hold at back, k2, sl 1 st from cable needle onto left needle and k this st, k2 from cable needle

sl 2 sts onto cable needle and hold at back, k3, then p2 from cable needle

sl 3 sts onto cable needle and hold at front, p2, then k3 from cable needle

sl 3 sts onto cable needle and hold at back, k3, then k3 from cable needle

sl 3 sts onto cable needle and hold at front, k3, then k3 from cable needle

k into front of 2nd st, k into back of first st, sl both sts off left needle together

k into front of 2nd st, p into front of first st, sl both sts off left needle together

k into back of 2nd st, k into front of first st, sl both sts off left needle together

p into back of 2nd st, k into front of first st, sl both sts off left needle together

k into front of 3rd st, then 2nd st, then first st, sl 3 sts off left needle together

k into front of 3rd st, p into front of first st, then 2nd st, sl 3 sts off needle together

p into back of 3rd st, then 2nd st, k into front of first st, sl 3 sts off left needle together

ABBREVIATIONS

inc	increase/increases/increasing
k	knit
kf&b	knit into front and then back of stitch
m1	make one stitch
m1L	make one stitch slanting left
m1R	make one stitch slanting right
p	purl
pf&b	purl into front and then back of stitch
rem	remaining
rep	repeat
RS	right side
skpo	sl 1 knitwise, k1, pass sl st over
sk2po	sl 1 knitwise, k2 tog, pass sl st over
sl	slip
ssk	sl first st and then 2nd st knitwise, insert left needle into sts and k2 tog
ssp	sl first st and then 2nd st purlwise, insert left needle into sts and p2 tog
st(s)	stitch(es)
tbl	through back of loop
tog	together
WS	wrong side
wyib	with yarn in back
wyif	with yarn in front
yfwd	yarn forward
yo	yarn over
[ ]	work instructions in brackets as directed

NEEDLE SIZES
The following is only a guide. The sizes are not always exact equivalents.

Metric (mm)	American	Old UK sizes
2	0	14
2.25	1	13
2.5	–	–
2.75	2	12
3	–	11
3.25	3	10
3.5	4	–
3.75	5	9
4	6	8
4.5	7	7
5	8	6
5.5	9	5
6	10	4
6.5	10½	3
7	–	2
7.5	–	1
8	11	0
9	13	00
10	15	000

GLOSSARY

Aran—sweater design with cables and textured stitch patterns in natural, cream wool; originally associated with the Aran Islands, Ireland, it can now simply refer to a design with cable patterns

Argyll—Scottish tartan sock pattern, now used to describe a diamond pattern with a superimposed plaid design

back (of work)—the side of the work away from the knitter

binding off—closing stitches at end of work

bobbin—(i) shape for winding on lengths of yarn, used for multicolored knitting; (ii) wooden tube with four pegs at top, used for 4-stitch tubular knitting

brushed—yarn with surface hairs raised in the manufacturing process

casting on—making stitches on needle at start of work

chart—(i) grid with colors or symbols representing motifs or stitch patterns; (ii) complete garment shape marked out on graph paper

crossed stitches—stitches worked through the back of the loops

eyelets—holes made with yarn overs and decreases; part of a lace stitch pattern

Fair Isle—distinctive patterns in stranded color knitting, originally associated with the Scottish island; now often used to describe many styles of multicolored knitting

faggot—lace stitch patterns using yarn overs and decreases on every row

front (of work)—the side of the work facing the knitter

garter stitch—basic stitch pattern; either knit every row or purl every row

gauge—(i) the number of stitches and rows to a given measurement, also known as tension; (ii) a device for measuring the size of knitting needles

knitwise—inserting needle into stitch as if to knit

man-made yarns—yarns from fibers made by chemical processes

multiple—a number of stitches grouped to form a repeat pattern along a row

natural fibers—animal hair, such as alpaca, mohair, or wool; plant fiber, such as cotton or linen

panel—a group of stitches forming a self-contained pattern

purlwise—inserting needle into stitch as if to purl

repeat—a group of stitches or rows worked more than once to form a pattern

right side—the side of the stitch pattern viewed when the item is complete

shaping—using increases to make the fabric wider or decreases to make the fabric narrower; these can be placed at the edges, along a row, or for a dart

stockinette stitch—basic stitch pattern; knit on right-side rows, purl on wrong-side rows

turning rows (short rows)—method of shaping by working part of a row, then turning the work

twisted stitches—stitches worked through the back of the loops; not to be confused with twist stitch patterns

wrong side—the side of the stitch pattern that will not be seen when the item is complete

INDEX

CREDITS

Quarto would like to thank and acknowledge the following for supplying pictures and items for photography reproduced in this book:

Jeanette Trottman for the bag on page 7, scarf on page 33, and mittens on page 50; Coats Crafts UK (www.coatscrafts.co.uk) for the equipment on pages 10–11; Betty Barnden for the sweater on page 50. The following items have been reproduced by kind permission of *Bella* magazine: mouse on page 39; cable sweater on page 80; child's Fair Isle jacket and beret on page 121. Thanks also to David Crawford for photographing the yarns on pages 12–13.

All other photographs and illustrations are the copyright of Quarto Publishing plc. While every effort has been made to credit contributors, Quarto would like to apologize should there have been any errors or omissions—and would be pleased to make the appropriate correction for future editions of the book.